THE PRE-RAPHAELITES
IN LITERATURE AND ART

OPENING PAGE OF "THE STORY OF THE
GLITTERING PLAIN"

The Pre-Raphaelites
in Literature
and Art

By

D. S. R. WELLAND Ph.D.

*With many illustrations
in half-tone and line*

Granger Index Reprint Series

BOOKS FOR LIBRARIES PRESS
FREEPORT, NEW YORK

First published 1953 as part of the
Life, Literature and Thought Library
by George G. Harrap & Co. Ltd.
Reprinted 1969 by arrangement

PR
466
W43
1969

STANDARD BOOK NUMBER:
8369-6046-7

LIBRARY OF CONGRESS CATALOG CARD NUMBER:
72-76949

MANUFACTURED
BY
HALLMARK LITHOGRAPHERS, INC.
IN THE U.S.A.

FOREWORD

THIS series aims at presenting in an attractive form English texts which have not only intrinsic merit as literature, but which are also valuable as manifestations of the spirit of the age in which they were written. The plan was inspired by the desire to break away from the usual annotated edition of English classics and to provide a series of books illustrating some of the chief developments in English civilization since the Middle Ages. Each volume will have a substantial introduction, which will relate the author to the main currents of contemporary life and thought, and which will be an important part of the book. Notes, where given, will be brief, stimulating, and designed to encourage the spirit of research in the student. It is believed that these books will be of especial value to students in universities and the upper forms of schools, and that they will also appeal very much to the general reader.

VIVIAN DE SOLA PINTO
General Editor

Life, Literature, and
Thought Library

ACKNOWLEDGMENTS

THE preparation of this volume has been greatly facilitated by the assistance I have received from the late Professor R. M. Hewitt, Professor V. de S. Pinto (the General Editor of this series), and Mr John Gere; I acknowledge with gratitude Professor Hewitt's stimulating suggestions and comments on Pre-Raphaelite literature, Professor Pinto's interest, advice, and help in every respect, and Mr Gere's kindness in supplying photographs for some illustrations and advising me on others.

I must also thank the many publishers, trustees of museums and art galleries, and private holders of copyright material, for their generosity in allowing me to reproduce poetry, prose, and illustrations in this volume. I have endeavoured to acknowledge each of them in detail at the appropriate place in the Notes, but I wish to offer my apologies to any who may have been inadvertently omitted.

D.S.R.W.

CONTENTS

THE CONTEMPORARY VIEW OF PRE-RAPHAELITISM

ILLUSTRATIONS
Plates in Half-tone

INTRODUCTION

ROBERT BUCHANAN, the bitterest opponent of Pre-Raphaelite ideals, committed himself to the generalization, "The truth is that literature, and more particularly poetry, is in a very bad way when one art gets hold of another, and imposes upon it its conditions and limitations." He is writing as a literary critic, and his prejudice is disclosed by the assertion that "Poetry is something more than painting." This fallacious value-comparison of the two arts, current in the Victorian period, is echoed by Oscar Wilde's opinion that the prose appreciations of Ruskin and Pater were greater than the pictures that inspired them:

> . . . greater, I always think, even as Literature is the greater art. Who, again, cares whether Mr Pater has put into the portrait of Monna Lisa something that Lionardo never dreamed of? . . . And so the picture becomes more wonderful to us than it really is, and reveals to us a secret of which, in truth, it knows nothing, and the music of the mystical prose is as sweet in our ears as was the flute-player's music that lent to the lips of La Gioconda those subtle and poisonous curves.

Ruskin on one occasion classifies painters in the belief that

> . . . a certain distinction must generally exist between men who, like Horace Vernet, David, or Domenico Tintoret, would employ themselves in painting, more or less graphically, the outward verities of passing events—battles, councils, etc.—of their day (who, supposing them to work worthily of their mission, would become, properly so called, historical or narrative painters); and men who sought, in scenes of perhaps less outward importance, "noble grounds for noble emotion";—who would be, in a separate sense, *poetical* painters, some of them

taking for subjects events which had actually happened, and others themes from the poets; or, better still, becoming poets themselves in the entire sense, and inventing the story as they painted it. Painting seems to me only just to be beginning, in this sense also, to take its proper position beside literature, and the pictures of the *Awakening Conscience*, *Huguenot*, and such others, to be the first fruits of its new effort.

Implicit in this is a characteristically Victorian moral judgement: literature is superior to painting in proportion to its greater power of creating "noble grounds for noble emotion," or, as Arnold put it, of "forming, sustaining and delighting us." Painting is seen as less capable of the positive, didactic communication of an uplifting moral message; it is thus an inferior art which must not be allowed to "get hold of" poetry.

Less inhibited than Buchanan by these moral considerations, we may be in a better position to seize the opportunity offered by the Pre-Raphaelites—unique in English literature except for Blake—of studying the inter-relationship between the two arts when both are practised concurrently by the same artists. Without Buchanan's prejudice, we may find that the inter-action of the two is more complex than the mere imposition upon poetry of the "conditions and limitations" of painting. It is a two-way process, and in many respects poetry gains more by it than does Pre-Raphaelite painting, which is often overburdened by excessive literariness. The poems, prose, and pictures collected in this volume have been chosen to facilitate such a comparison; they are not intended to give a comprehensive view of the work of each artist. Thus Morris's political tracts and pamphlets and Rossetti's translations are not included, while Swinburne is represented only by a handful of his earlier poems, showing his Pre-Raphaelite affinities most clearly. Prominence is given to Rossetti only because his work illustrates so well the interplay of the two media with its advantages and its limitations; the reader may remain in substantial agreement with the contemporary verdict that Rossetti was "an amateur who failed in two arts," but what matters is the imaginative boldness of his attempt to bring those two arts together and the effort it has had on his successors.

PRE-RAPHAELITE BOOK ILLUSTRATION

To attempt here a history of the Pre-Raphaelite movement is unnecessary—the bibliography indicates where accounts of this may be found—but the term 'Pre-Raphaelite' has acquired such width of reference that its present use must be defined. Employed with strictest accuracy, it can refer only to the seven members of the original Pre-Raphaelite Brotherhood founded by Holman Hunt, Millais, and D. G. Rossetti in 1848 and including, in addition to them, two other painters, F. G. Stephens and James Collinson, Thomas Woolner the sculptor, and Rossetti's brother, William Michael, the writer. Influenced by this group, although not formally members of it, were a number of other men such as Ford Madox Brown, William Bell Scott, W. H. Deverell, Arthur Hughes, and John Brett, whose aims and achievements in painting during the 1850's particularly were so close to those of the Brotherhood as to make artificial any attempt to differentiate between them in nomenclature, while the poets, Christina Rossetti and William Allingham, also deserve to be numbered with them as their friends, whose works they illustrated, and as the recipients of many valuable letters in which they discussed their beliefs and ideals. In some ways the group that gathered round Rossetti from 1857, comprising William Morris, Burne-Jones, and Swinburne, was much further removed from the original principles of Pre-Raphaelitism, especially as understood by Holman Hunt, and yet their choice of subject, their technique, and their interest in the fusion of art and literature make it desirable to include them also, though with certain reservations, in a selection of this nature.

It was, of course, in painting that Pre-Raphaelitism received its first impetus, and from art that it took its name, a nickname half jestingly applied to Hunt and Millais and adopted by them in a spirit of defiance. Dissatisfaction with what seemed to them the stereotyped artificiality of subject painting since Joshua Reynolds' Presidency of the Royal Academy at the end of the previous century had led them to seek their inspiration in a tradition other than that inaugurated by Raphael. Ruskin in *Modern Painters* had voiced a plea in 1843 for the introduction of motivating ideas into art, and this occurred also to the Pre-Raphaelites as a means of re-vitalizing subject-painting. Their insistence on every picture telling a story was the first step towards the affiliation of painting and literature and was to become even more important than their avowed adherence to Reynolds' neglected counsel of following nature. However perfunctory subject-painting may have become in the first half of the nineteenth century—and its unnaturalness has often been well-meaningly exaggerated—the landscape painting of Constable and Turner had followed nature closely enough to make Pre-Raphaelite naturalism less new than their literariness.

The pictures that best tell a story are book illustrations, and the favourite source for these was Shakespeare. Hunt's *Two Gentlemen of Verona*, Millais' *Death of Ophelia*, and Madox Brown's *Cordelia's Portion* are the best known, but Rossetti attempted many scenes, mostly from the tragedies, while Millais and Hughes both treated Ferdinand and Ariel in oils. Similarities of composition, particularly in the central figure, in these two pictures demonstrate the closeness of connection between the Pre-Raphaelites, as does the magnificent richness of colour in the skirts of Millais' *Mariana* and Hughes' *April Love*. After Shakespeare Keats was a fertile inspiration for Hunt's *Isabella*, Millais' fine *Lorenzo and Isabella* (which gains added interest by its use of members of the Brotherhood as models), and for minor works by others. Among contemporary poets they illustrated Browning and Edgar Allen Poe (especially in Rossetti's earliest period), Christina Rossetti, Allingham, and, most notably, Tennyson. The famous Moxon edition of his poems published in 1857 contained work by Millais, Hunt, and Rossetti, as well as other famous Victorian painters.

DORA

Sir J. E. Millais

Writing to Allingham in 1855 about this venture, Rossetti puts his finger on the chief danger of illustration:

I have not begun even designing for them yet, but fancy I shall try the *Vision of Sin*, and *Palace of Art*, etc.—those where one can allegorize on one's own hook, without killing for oneself and everyone a distinct idea of the poet's.

His designs for *The Palace of Art*, executed by the Dalziel brothers, have deservedly become classics of Victorian book illustration, for they have a spontaneity and originality that would have been impossible had he chosen such a poem as *Mariana*, which is pictorially complete in the Pre-Raphaelite manner as it stands:

> With blackest moss the flower-plots
>   Were thickly crusted, one and all:
> The rusted nails fell from the knots
>   That held the pear to the gable-wall.
> The broken sheds look'd sad and strange:
>   Unlifted was the clinking latch;
>   Weeded and worn the ancient thatch
> Upon the lonely moated grange.
>   She only said, 'My life is dreary,
>   He cometh not,' she said;
>   She said, 'I am aweary, aweary,
>   I would that I were dead!'

Richly pictorial poets do not lend themselves to illustration, and the Brotherhood's admiration for Tennyson and Keats shows itself more satisfactorily in their writing.

This desire to "allegorize on one's own hook" explains Rossetti's preference for Dante as a subject for illustration: time and again he turned to the theme of Dante and Beatrice, feeling a strong affinity with the poet whose name he bore and whose work he had studied and translated, and using the situations of that story as the vehicle for the communication of his own passionate intensity. Such works as his *Dantis Amor* and the celebrated *Beata Beatrix* are far more than illustrations: they have become expressions of a personal emotion and a mystical awareness of love that are enhanced by their literary reference instead of being subservient to it. Elizabeth Siddal is more than the model for Beatrice: she takes on the identity of Beatrice in these paintings in a wholly successful and deeply moving way, and here, far from cramping the painter's original genius, the literary subject has fired it and brought it to consummate perfection. Something of the same sort is true, though less unfailingly, of Rossetti's response to Arthurian themes.

The desire to allegorize is common to all the Pre-Raphaelites in their anxiety to transcend the limitations of illustration. Depicting an episode is not wholly the same thing as telling a story or expressing a motivating idea: to do this some machinery of reference is necessary, by which the rest of the story can be brought to the reader's mind, and this need they met by their use of significant details or "inventions" as they called them. Thus Millais' *Christ in the House of His Parents* (p. 161) is much more than the portrayal of an incident in the boyhood of Christ: the blood on the boy's injured palm that has dripped on to his foot prefigures the Crucifixion, just as the dove perched on a ladder at the back has a Pentecostal reference and the flock of shepherdless sheep outside the door extends still further the picture's allusiveness. Sometimes the method was employed with less subtlety than here, as in Rossetti's heraldically colourful *Wedding of St George and the Princess Sabra* where the earlier part of the story is indicated by the incongruous introduction into the bridal chamber of a grotesque dragon's head in a wooden box. Sometimes it is too subtle, as in Hunt's *The Hireling Shepherd* which can so easily be enjoyed as a sensuous study of bucolic courtship that the spectator may learn with some surprise of Hunt's conception of it as "a rebuke to the sectarian vanities and vital negligencies of the day," the shepherd representing "muddle-headed pastors."

Always the affinities between painting and writing were uppermost in their minds. If their painting was not an illustration to a piece of literature they would either compose a sonnet for their picture, as Rossetti did for *Found* and his two pictures of the Virgin and as Madox Brown did for *Work*, or they would elucidate the theme of a picture in prose comment, as Madox Brown also did for *Work* and as Holman Hunt did throughout his memoir. In January 1850 they brought out the first number of *The Germ*, a regrettably short-lived monthly which, in changing its title to *Art and Poetry* in March, defined its aim thus:

Of the little worthy the name of writing that has ever been written upon the principles of Art, (of course excepting that on the mere mechanism), a very small portion is by Artists themselves; and that is so scattered, that one scarcely knows where to find the ideas of an Artist except in his pictures.

With a view to obtain the thoughts of Artists, upon Nature as evolved in Art, in another language besides their *own proper* one, this Periodical has been established. Thus, then, it is not open to the conflicting opinions of all who handle the brush and palette, nor is it restricted to actual practitioners; but is intended to enunciate the principles of those who, in the true spirit of Art, enforce a rigid adherence to the simplicity of Nature either in Art or Poetry, and consequently regardless whether emanating from practical Artists, or from those who have studied nature in the Artist's School.

This is as near as the Pre-Raphaelites came to the publication of a manifesto except in F. G. Stephens' essay on "The Purpose and Tendency of Early Italian Art" in the second number of *The Germ*.

"The truth is that it is too good for the time. It is not *material* enough for the age," was the verdict of one reviewer upon the first two numbers. W. M. Rossetti, its editor, records that in November 1849 the Brotherhood "spoke of not admitting anything at all referring to politics or religion" into *The Germ*, and it is tempting to see this apparent indifference to social problems as the cause of its failure and as a besetting sin of the whole movement. Millais, whose early reputation as a boy-genius and whose facility of execution had brought a greater degree of popular recognition than the others had enjoyed, was soon turning out the accomplished, commercialized subject-pictures like *The Boyhood of Raleigh* and the *Bubbles* that became a soap-advertisement, pictures devoid of any reference to the world about him, but these are not Pre-Raphaelite in spirit at all. 'Escapist' as it has often been dubbed, the original Brotherhood was not as far removed from actuality as its detractors imply. The point merits some attention.

PRE-RAPHAELITISM AND CONTEMPORARY SOCIETY

The world into which Pre-Raphaelitism was born was far from pleasant. 1848 has been characterized as "the year of great and general revolt." At the beginning of the year there was serious apprehension of a French invasion. Then in February revolution broke out in Paris and Louis Philippe was overthrown. Rioting continued sporadically in France, and civil war raged in Hungary, in Austria, in Poland, and in Italy. This conflict of ideologies and classes throughout Europe is best epitomized by one fact: 1848 saw the publication of the Communist Manifesto by Karl Marx and Friedrich Engels. England was in the grip of the 'hungry forties': it was the aftermath of the Industrial Revolution, when working-class unrest had found expression in the Chartist risings. The panic-stricken fears of mob-violence that these aroused in higher levels of society had inspired *Barnaby Rudge* in 1841; they survive as the nightmare ideas of the Reign of Terror in *A Tale of Two Cities* (1859) and were still implicit ten years after that in Arnold's *Culture and Anarchy*. But domestic uneasiness was not only due to political causes: in 1848 the dangers of over-industrialization were emphasized in the grim form of an outbreak of cholera.

It is easy to criticize Millais' attitude, but less easy to define what the creative artist should be doing in the face of such events. Should he record them dispassionately, criticize them analytically, or ignore them entirely? On this point the Pre-Raphaelites, like all their contemporaries, were divided. W. M. Rossetti mentions a burlesque poem of his brother's, *The English Revolution of* 1848, which "ridicules the street-spoutings of Chartists and others in that year of vast continental upheavals." Twenty years were to elapse before the publication of William Morris's *The Earthly Paradise*, but some

familiar lines from that effectively indicate the æsthetic antidote
to the squalor, misery, and unrest of the time that Pre-Raphaelitism at its best represents:

> Forget six counties overhung with smoke,
> Forget the snorting steam and piston stroke,
> Forget the spreading of the hideous town;
> Think rather of the packhorse on the down,
> And dream of London, small, and white, and clean,
> The clear Thames bordered by its gardens green.

We are to forget the ugliness of mid-Victorian England, but
we are still to think of London—the idyllically purified London
of Morris's medieval dream-world or, in *News From Nowhere*,
the London that might follow the universal acceptance of
Morris's vision. The æstheticism of Rossetti and Burne-Jones
is not a creed of 'Art for Art's sake,' though in some ways they
anticipate the 1890's; rather is it a spirited reassertion of those
principles of colour, beauty, love, and cleanness that the drab,
agitated, discouraging world of the mid-nineteenth century
needed so much. It is more accurately defined as a protest
against existing conditions than as an escape from them, a
protest none the less sincere for the preference of some of its
exponents for a world of the æsthetic imagination.

Among the early Pre-Raphaelites the one whose paintings
are most clearly based on contemporary events was Ford
Madox Brown. *The Last of England* and its accompanying
sonnet comment on the prevalent emigrations, but more
important in this respect is the larger canvas *Work* (p. 97)
which celebrates the truly Victorian theme of honest toil.
Brown's sonnet for it begins with the lines:

> Work, which beads the brow and tans the flesh
> Of lusty manhood, casting out its devils,
> By whose weird art transmuting poor men's evils,
> Their bed seems down, their one dish ever fresh.

Unemployment is represented as the only evil, and the ex-
cavating labourers are held up for admiration as the pillars of

English society, while for the ragged, shifty-looking flower-collector in the left foreground our sympathy is invited in Brown's commentary as "the ragged wretch who has never been *taught* to *work*." Here again, for all its social comment, the genesis of the picture is incorrigibly literary. First-hand acquaintance with less-contented artisans might have disabused Brown of his conviction that employment was all that mattered to keep "their one dish ever fresh," but the picture leaves no doubt as to the source of that illusion. The two men in the right foreground, "the brainworkers" who "seeming to be idle, work, and are the cause of well-ordained work in others," are Thomas Carlyle and Frederick Denison Maurice. The ragged wretch has heedlessly passed a poster advertizing Maurice's Working Men's College, while the sandwich-men bear placards urging electoral support for Bobus. The identity of Bobus is to be traced to Chapter IV of the Proem to Carlyle's *Past and Present*, where he is a "Sausage-maker on the great scale . . . with his cash accounts and larders dropping fatness, with his respectabilities, warm garnitures, and pony chaise," the Victorian bourgeois capitalist who is always "raising such a clamour for this Aristocracy of Talent" which Carlyle demonstrates as non-existent. Small wonder that Rossetti described *Work* as full of "all kinds of Carlylianisms," for this doctrine of the blessedness of work even if it means the renunciation of happiness is the Everlasting Yea of *Sartor Resartus*:

> Close thy *Byron*; open thy *Goethe*. . . . there is in man a *higher* than Love of Happiness: he can do without Happiness, and instead thereof find Blessedness! . . . Most true is it, as a wise man teaches us, that "Doubt of any sort cannot be removed except by Action" . . . Produce! Produce! Were it but the pitifulest infinitesimal fraction of a Product, produce it in God's name! 'Tis the utmost thou hast in thee: out with it then. Up, up! Whatsoever thy hand findeth to do, do it with thy whole might.

To the modern reader there is a certain unreality in this

shrilly-enunciated doctrine, and that unreality is intensified when it is retailed to us second-hand in Brown's painting, for all its technical interest. The doctrine was, moreover, being questioned even when the picture was being painted (1852–1865), for in 1851 Ruskin had begun his pamphlet *Pre-Raphaelitism* with the words:

> It may be proved, with much certainty, that God intends no man to live in this world without working: but it seems to me no less evident that He intends every man to be happy in his work.

That this is closer to the belief of the other Pre-Raphaelites may be shown by the juxtaposition of this passage written by Morris in a pamphlet in 1887:

> Therefore the Aim of Art is to increase the happiness of men, by giving them beauty and interest of incident to amuse their leisure, and prevent them wearying even of rest, and by giving them hope and bodily pleasure in their work; or, shortly, to make man's work happy and his rest fruitful.

Morris goes on to point out that "art is, and must be, either in its abundance or its barrenness, in its sincerity or its hollowness, the expression of the society amongst which it exists." It is on that realization that all his later work is founded, for his preoccupation with the dream-world of romance had led him back inexorably to the society of the present, about which he knew far more and knew it more realistically than ever Carlyle did.

Some awareness of the limitations of Carlyle's influence is perhaps implicit in *Work*, for, speaking of the rich man on the horse, Brown writes:

> . . . could he only be got to hear what the sages in the corner have to say, I have no doubt he would be easily won over. But the road is blocked . . .

Does Brown intend, in the composition of his picture, to hint at the inability of the Carlyles and the Maurices to establish contact with the upper, influential classes of society? The commentary does not increase our enjoyment of the picture even if it extends our understanding by revealing the unsuspected complexity of its potential 'messages.' Pleasing as the design is, it may be that Brown attempts too much in it and allows social significance to interfere with its æsthetic appeal. Even his grandson, usually staunch in his admiration, complains that it is "difficult for the eye to find a point on which to settle."

The concluding pages of Holman Hunt's *Pre-Raphaelitism and the Pre-Raphaelite Brotherhood* show his recognition of the relation between art and society, but show too that he thought of that relation in moral terms:

> All art from the beginning served for the higher development of men's minds. It has ever been valued as food to sustain strength for noble resolves, not as that devoured by epicures only to surfeit the palate.

The Awakened Conscience (p. 96) is Hunt's best practical expression of this belief, and like many other Pre-Raphaelite pictures its morality has a dual source of literary inspiration in the Bible and in contemporary writing:

> When *The Light of the World* was on my easel at Chelsea in 1851, it occurred to me that my spiritual subject called for a material counterpart in a picture representing in actual life the manner in which the appeal of the spirit of heavenly love calls a soul to abandon a lower life. In reading *David Copperfield* I had been deeply touched by the pathos of the search by old Peggotty after little Emily, when she had become an outcast, and I went about to different haunts of fallen girls to find a locality suitable for the scene of the old mariner's pursuing love. My object was not to illustrate any special incident in the book, but to take the suggestion of the loving seeker of the fallen girl coming upon the object of his search. I spoke freely of this intended subject, but, while cogitating upon the broad intention, I reflected that the instinctive eluding of pursuit by the erring one would not coincide with the willing conversion and instantaneous resolve for a higher life which it was necessary to emphasise.

As Hunt himself points out, the theme of the lover finding his former sweetheart as a prostitute was treated by Rossetti pictorially and in sonnet form under the title *Found* (p. 113). The drawing for the never-completed oil painting is an excellent example of his draughtsmanship, but Hunt is right in seeing that this situation lends itself to pathos and pity rather than to the moral earnestness at which Hunt aimed: it remains a moving, human story, which is how the twentieth century will see many of these pictures, finding their didacticism embarrassingly over-emphasized. The sonnet, with its Keats quotation, sentimentalizes the subject far more than the drawing does. Hunt continues:

> While recognising this, I fell upon the text in Proverbs, "As he that taketh away a garment in cold weather, so is he that singeth songs to a heavy heart." These words, expressing the unintended stirring up of the deeps of pure affection by the idle sing-song of an empty mind, led me to see how the companion of the girl's fall might himself be the unconscious utterer of a divine message. In scribbles I arranged the two figures to present the woman recalling the memory of her childish home, and breaking away from her gilded cage with a startled holy resolve, while her shallow companion still sings on, ignorantly intensifying her repentant purpose.

In characteristic Pre-Raphaelite manner the moral of this picture is underlined by 'inventions': the cruelty of the human situation is copied in the cat who plays beneath the table with a maimed and dying bird, the discarded glove suggests the eventual discarding of the mistress by the seducer, the freshness of the mirrored garden scene contrasts with the oppressive luxury of the interior of gilded iniquity. Ruskin exclaimed with enthusiasm:

> There is not a single object in all that room—common, modern, vulgar (in the vulgar sense, as it may be), but it becomes tragical, if rightly read . . . nay, the very hem of the poor girl's dress, at which the painter has laboured so closely, thread by

thread, has story in it, if we think how soon its pure whiteness
may be soiled with dust and rain, her outcast feet failing in the
street.

This is allowing the fancy excessive liberty, but Hunt and the
Brotherhood must have approved wholeheartedly this way of
"reading" a picture for the "story in it." Yet, valuable as these
contributory factors are, the real key to the situation so
dramatically presented is a literary one, and is to be found in
the title of the song on the music-rest: it is Thomas Moore's
Oft in the Stilly Night, the nostalgic fragrance of which is in
perfect harmony with the picture's mood and evokes the sen-
timentalism that Hunt manages to stiffen with his moral comment:

> Oft in the stilly night,
>   Ere slumber's chain has bound me,
> Fond Memory brings the light
>   Of other days around me:
>   The smiles, the tears
>   Of boyhood's years,
>   The words of love then spoken;
>   The eyes that shone,
>   Now dimm'd and gone,
>   The cheerful hearts now broken!

There is also a roll of music in the case on the floor in the left
foreground, and from what is visible of its title it would appear
to be a setting of Tennyson's *Tears, Idle Tears*, a lyric that had
been published in *The Princess* only five years before Hunt
began work on *The Awakened Conscience*, but which, for the
spectator who has the familiarity with it that Hunt expected,
epitomizes the mood and heightens the poignancy of the situation very effectively:

> Tears, idle tears, I know not what they mean,
> Tears from the depth of some divine despair
> Rise in the heart and gather to the eyes,

.   .   .   .

> Dear as remember'd kisses after death,
> And sweet as those by hopeless fancy feign'd
> On lips that are for others; deep as love,
> Deep as first love, and wild with all regret;
> Oh Death in Life, the days that are no more.

The whole passage has a striking relevance to the picture, yet it is only incidentally introduced into it and might easily be overlooked.

If *The Awakened Conscience* is a literary painting, a poem that challenges comparison with it, Rossetti's *Jenny*, is essentially the product of a painter, despite the literary suggestion of its Shakespearian epigraph. Less Browningesque than *A Last Confession*, it has a sincerity and individuality, and a kindly tolerance not wholly to be expected of that time. What is admirable is the alternation between sentiment and realism, between a warm sympathy for the individual and an involuntary shrinking from the degradation she embodies, as well as the suspicion of moral judgment which still does not condone the way of life, and the tempering of romanticism with quiet irony in such lines as

> Poor shameful Jenny, full of grace
> Thus with your head upon my knee;
> Whose person or whose purse may be
> The lodestar of your reverie?

The complexity of the attitude to the prostitute is true to life; the method of presentation and its unforcedly easy colloquial manner suggest the actual process of thought. Dramatic as it is, a scene like this is unmistakably a painter's composition, and a Pre-Raphaelite painter's:

> Why, there's the dawn!
>
> And there's an early waggon drawn
> To market, and some sheep that jog
> Bleating before a barking dog;
> And the old streets come peering through
> Another night that London knew;
> And all as ghost-like as the lamps.

So on the wings of day decamps
My last night's frolic. Glooms begin
To shiver off as lights creep in
Past the gauze curtains half drawn-to,
And the lamp's doubled shade grows blue,
Your lamp, my Jenny, kept alight
Like a wise virgin's, all one night!
And in the alcove coolly spread
Glimmers with dawn your empty bed;
And yonder your fair face I see
Reflected lying on my knee,
Where teems with faint foreshadowings
Your pier-glass scrawled with diamond rings:
And on your bosom all night worn
Yesterday's rose now droops forlorn,
But dies not yet this summer morn.

And now without, as if some word
Had called upon them that they heard,
The London sparrows far and nigh
Clamour together suddenly;
And Jenny's cage-bird grown awake.
Here in their song his part must take,
Because here too the day doth break.

The convenient placing of a mirror so that the reflected image
can play its part in the picture recalls the Dutch school, but
it will be found similarly used in Madox Brown's unfinished
Take your son, Sir!, in Holman Hunt's *Lady of Shalott*, and, more
significantly, in *The Awakened Conscience*. There is the painter's
eye for light and the same dramatic use of the cold greyness of
dawn that was to have set the keynote of *Found* with its subject
so similar to this—"London's smokeless resurrection light,"
as he described it in the sonnet—and the sheep in this passage
are fulfilling a symbolic function similar to that of the tied calf
in *Found* as well as recalling the market references elsewhere in
Jenny. Here, too, are all the other 'inventions' that would have
had their place in a painting of the scene: the lamp still alight
(with an ironical glancing Biblical allusion), the drooping rose

which also has its relation to the flower-imagery throughout, and the caged bird singing because he must. If these things recall *The Awakened Conscience*, so too does the device of using the purity of external nature to contrast with the impurity within: there it was the reflected garden, here it is the London sparrows and the drooping rose. One of the most felicitous instances of the complete fusion of painting and poetry, this is the key passage in the poem and it gains greatly from the pictorial associations it evokes.

This theme of the fallen woman had a peculiar attraction for the Pre-Raphaelites. Hunt devotes a good deal of time to demonstrating that *The Awakened Conscience* was complete before *Found* was begun, Ruskin's correspondence with Rossetti belies it, while William Bell Scott in his *Autobiographical Notes* asserts that *Found* was first thought of as an illustration to his own *Rosabell*, a poetically uneven product of what Buchanan would have called the "sub-Tennysonian school." Which of these came first is a matter of minor importance; more worthy of attention is their common interest in the theme. That one source of this is moral has been seen already, but Millais' pen-and-ink *Retribution* (p. 145), with its sharply delineated agonizing conflict of emotion, by changing the setting throws fresh light on the subject. Here the seducer is confronted in the presence of his horrified wife and curious maidservant by his mistress and their illegitimate children, and illicit sexual relations are denounced for their violation of the sanctity of the home. The Victorian apotheosis of the domestic virtues was at its height at this time. The year 1854, which saw the exhibiting of *The Awakened Conscience*, is the date of *Retribution* and also of the beginning of Coventry Patmore's *The Angel in the House*. Already art was being assessed by its suitability for family consumption; family fiction was established, and Trollope had begun the writing of those novels for which he was later to claim with pride, "I do believe that no girl has risen from the reading of my pages less modest than she was before"; while in music the forms most characteristic of the age were the piano solo and the sentimental ballad—domestic forms, simple enough for convincing amateur performance and not over-subtle in their emotional appeal. The works of the Pre-Raphaelites and of Patmore, which, as might be expected, had much in common, had the necessary probity to constitute family literature. In his novel, *The Unclassed* (1884), George Gissing allows Waymark to recommend to Maud Enderby at a particular crisis in her emotional development the poems of Rossetti:

> These gave her much help in restoring her mind to quietness. Their perfect beauty entranced her, and the rapturous purity of ideal passion, the mystic delicacies of emotion, which made every verse gleam like a star, held her for the time high above that gloomy cloudland of her being, rife with weird shapes and muffled voices. . . . Rossetti put into utterance for her so much that she had not dared to entrust even to the voice of thought.

Similarly, as late as 1903 in *Man and Superman* Jack Tanner declines in advance "the copies of Patmore's *Angel in the House* in extra morocco" which it was still fashionable to give as wedding presents.

Yet the Pre-Raphaelite treatment of the theme of the fallen woman is not to be attributed solely to a moral championing of marital fidelity. Their paintings show a marked interest in *Measure for Measure*, the play of which Pater was to write so sympathetically later, and for them as for Angelo the sin they denounce has its fascination. Pulling against Victorian morality was the Romantic delight in passion, and it was this passion to which an illogical prudery denied artistic expression even in a conjugal setting. Patmore was accepted only because he sublimated passion into something more ethereal, and when Rossetti's *House of Life* was published in 1870 the outcry against the sonnet *Nuptial Sleep* was so great as to force its suppression. At the same time the "discreet establishment" was receiving greater publicity from social opprobrium than it had had in the past when its existence had been tacitly ignored, and as Angelo's desire for Isabella was stimulated by his moral indignation against Claudio, so the Pre-Raphaelites became even more conscious of the irrational power of sexual attraction in a society that strove to repress it. Much of their work is characterized by a pent-up passion struggling to confine itself within the romantically idealized bounds of Arthur Hughes's delicate and fragrant *April Love*, in the sentimentalized frustration of his *Long Engagement*, or in the allegorical form of *The Hireling Shepherd*, until here again the cult of medievalism came to the rescue. The convention of courtly love made it possible for William Morris to undertake the *Defence of Guenevere*, the literary associations and background allowed Rossetti to paint the story of Paolo and Francesca as well as the Guinevere theme, and, most valuable of all, gave him in the figures of Dante and Beatrice the perfect symbolic expression of his deepest emotions.

DETAIL IN PRE-RAPHAELITE DESCRIPTION

It was not only the fragile, spiritual beauty of an Elizabeth Siddal that moved Rossetti. Some of his other "stunners" (the word is his own) were of a more sensuous type, and it was his portraying of women such as the Fanny Cornforth of *Found* and the strikingly lovely Jane Morris, wife of the poet, that earned the charge of "fleshliness" from Buchanan. His treatment of these is characterized by the curving rhythmic grace he imparts to them by his accentuation of rich auburn hair, the lushness of the lips, and the stately sweep of the long neck, as well as the sultry use of colour in oils like *Proserpine* or the quite differently bold and brilliant use of it in the luxuriant *The Beloved*. The pose with the head thrown back and the neck elongated, the hair falling in profusion on the shoulders and the eyes charged with emotional intensity, was used so often as to make parody inevitable, and no one could have parodied it less maliciously or more effectively than Max Beerbohm in *Poets' Corner*. Yet Rossetti achieved some remarkably powerful effects from it in words as well as in line. The passage from *A Last Confession* (p. 98) demands comparison with the exquisite pen and ink study of Mrs Morris (p. 144): the imagery, the loving detail, and the whole tone is so evocative of the picture as to make the two complementary. Everything is visualized pictorially, and the closing lines extend the portrait into a minute but perfectly drawn landscape where again the light is as important and as clearly defined as it was in *Jenny*.

Throughout his poetry Rossetti instinctively describes in pictorial terms anything that his imagination seizes on. It is not a question of "one art getting hold of another" and imposing "upon it its conditions and limitations" so much as of a gifted artist transferring unconsciously to one medium the means of expression he would have used in another. This description of a sick-bed vigil from *My Sister's Sleep* is an example:

> Twelve struck. That sound, by dwindling years
>   Heard in each hour, crept off; and then
>   The ruffled silence spread again,
> Like water that a pebble stirs.
>
> Our mother rose from where she sat;
>   Her needles, as she laid them down,
>   Met lightly, and her silken gown
> Settled: no other noise than that.

Sounds here are described entirely in terms of visual imagery: the sound *crept* off, the *ruffled* silence spreads like the ripples of a pool, and in the second stanza the noises are not suggested by onomatopaeic words like 'clicked' or 'rustled,' but the actual movement is described as it would be seen, and the reader, visualizing it, supplies the sound himself. Again, the sonnet *Silent Noon* (p. 100) may be compared, if we make allowances for the erotic atmosphere present only in the poem, with

Millais' *The Blind Girl*, which Rossetti described as "one of the most touching and perfect things I know." Both have the same sensuous quality, the same fullness of colour, the same detailed accuracy of observation. The butterfly on the blind girl's shawl is unmistakably a Red Admiral; there is the same exactness of reference in the flower descriptions of the sonnet. Her blindness is touchingly brought out by the way in which she fingers the blades of grass; there is a parallel in the tactile imagery with which the sonnet opens, while both picture and sonnet are excellently epitomized by the telling pictorial phrase "visible silence, still as the hour-glass."

This interchange of ideas and manner between artists was one of the most striking features of the early Brotherhood. Both Rossetti and Millais caught something of Hunt's moral fervour, and drawings such as *Retribution*, *The Ghost*, and *The Race-Meeting* suggest in Millais the potentiality of a moral artist of some power. Hunt in his turn was influenced by Rossetti's sensuousness, while contact with Millais, unquestionably the most accomplished of them technically, must have improved both Hunt's and Rossetti's craftsmanship and encouraged their treatment of detail. It is in this respect that they followed Nature, in their meticulous concentration on the accuracy of every detail. The wood shavings on the floor of *The Carpenter's Shop* still evoke admiration for their execution and observation; the flowers and foliage that surround the drowning Ophelia are botanically correct, and the background to *The Blind Girl* is recognizably Winchelsea. Bell Scott records Millais, in about 1850, commenting to him on the elaborate detail of an Italian engraving: "That's P.R.B. enough, is it not? We haven't come up to that yet. But I for one won't try: it's all nonsense; of course nature's nature, and art's art, isn't it? One could not live doing that," but Millais did live by doing something very close to that for many years and so did the others, so that Scott is over-hasty in observing, "So soon had the principal executive tenet of the bond fallen

off." Their desire for authenticity led them to a quest for
models that would often be laughable were it not inspired by
such seriousness of purpose. Only a carpenter could serve
Millais as a model for Joseph to ensure correct muscular
development; Hunt, revolving the idea of a Little Emily

LOCKSLEY HALL
Sir J. E. Millais

picture, sought an appropriate background among the haunts
of fallen women, and his arrangements for nocturnal work on
The Light of the World in order to get the right blend of light
and shade were equally elaborate, while the posing of Miss
Siddal as Ophelia in a bath of water heated by an oil-lamp
nearly had serious consequences. Whether all this is attributable,
as Scott suggests, to the indirect influence of the Daguerrotype,

invented a few years earlier, is debatable. They may have been anxious to demonstrate that science and the camera could do nothing that could not be done as well or better by a skilled craftsman with a brush. On the other hand it was an age given to leisureliness in art and taught by the development of scientific knowledge to demand fidelity to nature as a proof of excellence and to equate thoroughness with sincerity of purpose. The same absorption with detail is apparent in fiction and was later to find its way on to the stage in the vogue for detailed realism of setting that followed the success of T. W. Robertson's *Caste* in 1867.

In literature this concern with detail was valuable because wise selection ensured the use only of significant detail; in pictorial art this meticulousness was of more questionable value. Thus *The Death of Ophelia* has been described as an instance of 'consecutive vision,' each detail being painted in with an exactness only possible if the artist were standing opposite to each piece of foliage simultaneously: in other words, the spectator is encouraged, as with *Work*, to a piece-by-piece approach to the picture rather than to a whole, focused view of it. It is thus that one is tempted to study the *Ramsgate Sands* or *Derby Day* of Frith, but as Frith is not concerned with the communication of a moral it matters less there. Ruskin, defending *The Awakened Conscience* in *The Times*, anticipated this objection:

> But I can easily understand that to many persons the careful rendering of the inferior details in this picture cannot but be at first offensive, as calling their attention away from the principal subject. It is true that detail of this kind has long been so carelessly rendered, that the perfect finishing of it becomes a matter of curiosity, and therefore an interruption to serious thought. But without entering into the question of the general propriety of such treatment, I would only observe that, at least in this instance, it is based on a truer principle of the pathetic than any of the common artistical expedients of the schools. Nothing is more

notable than the way in which even the most trivial objects force themselves upon the attention of a mind which has been fevered by violent and distressful excitement. They thrust themselves forward with a ghastly and unendurable distinctness, as if they would compel the sufferer to count, or measure, or learn them by heart. Even to the mere spectator a strange interest exalts the accessories of a scene in which he bears witness to human sorrow.

True as this is, it remains a piece of special pleading not applicable to other pictures where the fussiness of detail can be distracting, although in the landscape work of Brown and in the backgrounds of Hunt, Millais, and Hughes that detail does contribute in no small way to the hard clarity of light in which they saw the world about them and which gave their work another of its distinguishing features.

As we see it, Pre-Raphaelite painting gives the imagination far too little to do, and indeed much of it could be adduced as evidence of a mid-Victorian deficiency of imagination. The use of 'inventions' offsets this in some ways, although even with these it is the imagination of the painter that is exercised primarily, and the spectator is asked to use his intellect. All the clues are painstakingly given to us, and we are left to piece them together in our mind to arrive at an understanding of the picture's message. The technique, though less subtly and less ironically employed, is analogous to the method of literary allusion with which the poetry of T. S. Eliot has familiarized the modern reader, and if the pictures are sometimes open to the same objection as that poetry—"what right has he to expect us to have read these things or to see his inference?" —it is open also to the same answer. Poetry is not the only art that can communicate before it is understood, and there are few Pre-Raphaelite paintings that do not make some immediate appeal to the spectator as pictures by virtue of their composition or their use of colour even before the various allusions have been intellectually apprehended. Rossetti, the most literary of them all, proves that Pre-Raphaelitism need not lead, as it did with Millais, to popular facility and over-obviousness. It is for the imaginative strength of his poetry and painting that Rossetti is remarkable, for the *minutiæ* of his work are managed with too much skill to deaden the reader's response. It would have been too much to expect the original Brotherhood to maintain over many years their relationship of interaction, idealism, and co-ordination of viewpoint; when it did begin to disintegrate, although Hunt remained closest to its original tenets, it was the mercurial, colourful personality of Rossetti that found new disciples and his ideas that gained such currency as to lead people still to speak of Pre-Raphaelite qualities when it is pre-eminently to the idiosyncrasies of Rossetti that they refer.

PRE-RAPHAELITE MEDIEVALISM

In the second phase of Pre-Raphaelitism the functions of painter and writer were not combined in the same person (except of course for Rossetti), since Morris did little painting or drawing except for his decorative work, and Burne-Jones was not a man of letters. The medievalism popularly associated with Pre-Raphaelitism, a manifestation rather of this later phase than of the original Brotherhood, is the only aspect of it requiring comment. Rossetti's veneration for Dante remained personal to him but his delight in Arthurian legend was shared by the others, and it was the ill-fated, because technically inexpert, attempt in 1857 to translate that delight into murals for the Oxford Union that first brought Rossetti, Morris, and Burne-Jones into active co-operation. Again Rossetti dominated the group. Burne-Jones's interest had been aroused by Rossetti's illustration for Allingham's *The Maids of Elfin Mere*, and Morris, who had already acquired a love of Chaucer, the ballads, and the medieval world of his imagination, was ready to surrender to this exciting, exotic personality. For them medievalism began as an escape from the constricting drabness of the contemporary world. Hunt and Madox Brown would not without protest have allowed the term Pre-Raphaelite to be applied to lines such as these:

> Dreamer of dreams, born out of my due time,
> Why should I strive to set the crooked straight?
> Let it suffice me that my murmuring rhyme
> Beats with light wing against the ivory gate.

For Burne-Jones the Middle Ages was essentially "such stuff as dreams are made on," and his pictures of it are coloured by "a light that never was on sea or land," so that at times it becomes little more than an irritating affectation—"Wardour Street medieval," as one modern critic has not undeservedly called *King Cophetua and the Beggar Maid*.

Despite a technical skill far in excess of Rossetti's, some of Burne-Jones's etherealized and emasculated paintings have an insipidity that Rossetti usually avoids, but Rossetti, Burne-Jones, and Morris were all capable of a spurious medievalism that rings particularly hollow against their more genuine work. The contrast is shown felicitously by two sentences from Morris's *The Water of the Wondrous Isles*. The romance opens on a note of debased pastiche:

> Whilom, as tells the tale, was a walled cheaping-town hight Utterhay, which was builded in a bight of the land a little off the great highway which went from over the mountains to the sea.

This pales quickly before the virile directness and poetic dignity of the fine passage that closes the tale:

> Now when all this hath been said, we have no more to tell about this company of friends, the most of whom had once haunted the lands about the Water of the Wondrous Isles, save that their love never sundered, and that they lived without shame and died without fear. So here is an end.

If the first recalls some of Burne-Jones's paintings, it recalls also the pseudo-medievalism of much Victorian architecture and the affectation that Browning pilloried in his "Middle-

Age-manners-adapter" of *The Flight of the Duchess*. The second passage has more in common with the admirable directness of some of Burne-Jones's drawings. This contrast between his paintings and his drawings is not wholly accounted for by the difference of medium, because many of his oils and water-colours are unquestionably fine, but in medieval subjects he seems better able to discipline his fancy in line. The drawings from the Kelmscott Chaucer (*frontis.*) and the early *Going to the Battle*, with its wealth of carefully executed decorative detail, have a freshness and individuality that become hackneyed in the larger works; his illustrations for Chaucer, vividly realized and clean in their outlines, have a happy appropriateness, whereas in his *Love among the Ruins* the painter's medievalizing habit has lost the exhilaration of Browning's poem and blunted the contrast of the poet's juxtaposition of modern and antique in a scene that is closer to the amphitheatre scene in *The Mayor of Casterbridge* than to Burne-Jones's picture. It is as the decorative artist of tapestry and stained glass, and as the illustrator of Chaucer that Burne-Jones's affinities with the original conception of the Pre-Raphaelites are seen to best advantage, for there literature furnishes motivating ideas for works of art which are nevertheless well capable of standing alone.

The link between painting and literature was maintained in their treatment of medieval subjects, as may be seen from the pictorial quality of Morris's prose and poetry as a whole, of which this extract from the romance *Golden Wings* is representative:

> Then I said to her "Now, O Love, we must part for a little; it is time for me to go and die."
>
> "Why should you go away?" she said, "they will come here quick enough, no doubt, and I shall have you longer with me if you stay; I do not turn sick at the sight of blood." . . . She threw herself down and kissed my feet, and then did not get up at once but lay there holding my feet. And while she lay there, behold a

sudden tramping that she did not hear, and over the green
hangings the gleam of helmets that she did not see, and then one
pushed aside the hangings with his spear, and there stood the
armed men. "Will not somebody weep for my darling?" She
sprung up from my feet with a low bitter moan, most terrible to
hear, she kissed me once on the lips, and then stood aside, with

TROILUS AND CRISEYDE
Sir E. Burne-Jones

her dear head thrown back, and holding her lovely loose hair
strained over her outspread arms as though she were wearied of
all things that had been or that might be.

The pose is that of a Pre-Raphaelite picture, and the situation
and mood of this passage are remarkably similar to Rossetti's
drawing of *Launcelot in the Queen's Chamber* (p. 160).

The work of Burne-Jones and Morris at its best re-estab-
lished the link between art and society that Rossetti's subjective

mysticism had weakened at times, and, in re-establishing it, widened it from being purely moral as with Holman Hunt into something æsthetic and yet practical. Morris's designs for furniture and furnishings put into practice his own dictum: "Have nothing in your houses that you do not know to be useful, or believe to be beautiful." Designs and dictum alike combine the æsthetic with the realistic just as the medieval imaginary world of *The Haystack in the Floods* is brought to life by its touches of realistic detail, and just as Pre-Raphaelite painting has always tried to temper escapist beauty with factual observation. Dissatisfaction with the drabness and dirt of Victorian England made Morris a Pre-Raphaelite, and Pre-Raphaelitism led him to an artistic re-statement of the principles necessary to the revitalization of that England and to an active awareness of the craftsmanship by which he could contribute to that revitalization.

To say that a more sparing use of literary apparatus would have entitled the Pre-Raphaelites' pictures to be ranked more highly as art may be true. Sir Thomas Bodkin dismisses them for having "helped to spread the pernicious contagion" of "anecdotage" and an "unhappy insistence upon extraneous illustrative matter"; he considers that "none of these efforts illumined the writer's work, and few of them had valid claims to justify their independent existence," and speaks of "the moral or didactic implications which always follow on conscious illustration." From the viewpoint of the art connoisseur the objection is understandable, but it underestimates the pressure of the spirit of the age. In Holman Hunt and Madox Brown, as well as in the others to a lesser extent, moral didacticism did not "follow on conscious illustration": it was the motivation of their work, and the literariness of their painting is the outcome of it, the best means to hand of making art serve their moral purpose. From an historical estimate, their art did what their age required of it, and although it is not without intrinsic merit it remains the product of a particular age.

In painting, the moral realism and clarity of colour that distinguished Pre-Raphaelitism were soon to give way to the Impressionism that aimed primarily at the communication of pleasure and at the avoidance of sharp definition of outline, but the art of the Brotherhood was to influence English literature for several decades. The young W. B. Yeats found a strong poetic stimulus in their æstheticism, their love of a legendary past, and their craftsmanship. Bernard Shaw, undeterred by the fact that their art was moral and didactic (he might have applied to it his comment on the reception of *Pygmalion*: "It goes to prove my contention that great art can never be anything else"), tried in *Candida* to write "a modern Pre-Raphaelite play." The Pre-Raphaelites fired the imagination of many writers of Edwardian England, and of none more than the young D. H. Lawrence. He wrote to a friend in 1910: "Somewhere I have got the ballad of *Sister Helen*—Rossetti's—beating time. I couldn't repeat it, but yet I beat through the whole poem with now and then a refrain cropping up." By 1929 their spell was less strong because of their attitude to sex, and in the "Introduction to his Paintings" he writes, "As far as I am concerned, the Pre-Raphaelites don't exist," but there is no doubt that they existed vividly for him when he wrote his early poems, and such novels as *The White Peacock* (1911) are markedly Pre-Raphaelite, especially in their descriptive passages.

The Pre-Raphaelites were symptomatic of the leisured culture that largely disappeared with the Great War, and their didactic earnestness has not always been to the taste of later generations (although the exhibitions and publications occasioned by their centenary in 1948 indicate a renewal of interest in them). An exhibition before the first war moved Isaac Rosenberg, himself a painter-poet of promise, to a critical essay on the relationship between the two arts, with a quotation from which this introduction can usefully end:

We are apt to confuse imagination with literature, with the psychological interest of a picture, as a quality apart from its technical qualities. Literature, I think, is permissible if it enhances the interest of a picture, but it only increases the difficulties of imagination. A picture must be a perfect consistency of thought and execution, of colour and design and conception; the more dramatic or psychological a picture is the more intense must be the imagination of colour and design to harmonise with the idea. The psychology is helpless without the other elements; the psychology itself is only part of the imagination and perhaps the smallest. Whatever the subject, nature is always our resort, a basis for creation. To feel and interpret nature, to project ourself beyond nature through nature, and yet convince of our faithfulness to the sensation, is imagination.

The ultimate end of all the arts should be beauty. Poetry and music achieve that end through the intellect and the ear, painting and sculpture through the eye. The former possess advantages which the latter do not; and the latter *vice versa*. Painting is stationary while poetry is in motion. Through the intellect the emotion is enchained; feeling made articulate transmits its exact state to the reader. Each word adapts itself to the phase of emotion (I include sensation of the soul), and carries one along from degree to degree. Painting can only give the moment, the visual aspect, and only suggest the spiritual consciousness; not even a mood, but the phase of a mood. By imagination in paint we do not encroach on the domain of the writer; we give what the writer cannot give, with all his advantages, the visible aspect of things, which the writer can only suggest, and give that aspect a poetic interest; and by that a more intensely human interest: for here the body and the soul are one, and beauty the crown thereof.

PRE-RAPHAELITE WRITINGS ON ART

F. G. STEPHENS

THE PURPOSE AND TENDENCY OF EARLY ITALIAN ART

THE object we have proposed to ourselves in writing on Art, has been "an endeavour to encourage and enforce an entire adherence to the simplicity of nature; and also to direct attention, as an auxiliary medium, to the comparatively few works which Art has yet produced in this spirit." It is in accordance with the former and more prominent of these objects that the writer proposes at present to treat.

An unprejudiced spectator of the recent progress and main direction of Art in England will have observed, as a great change in the character of the productions of the modern school, a marked attempt to lead the taste of the public into a new channel by producing pure transcripts and faithful studies from nature, instead of conventionalities and feeble reminiscences from the Old Masters; an entire seeking after originality in a more humble manner than has been practised since the decline of Italian Art in the Middle Ages. This has been most strongly shown by the landscape painters, among whom there are many who have raised an entirely new school of natural painting, and whose productions undoubtedly surpass all others in the simple attention to nature in detail as well as in generalities. By this they have succeeded in earning for themselves the reputation of being the finest landscape painters in Europe. But although this success has been great and merited, it is not of them that we have at present to treat, but rather to recommend their example to their fellow-labourers, the historical painters.

That the system of study to which this would necessarily lead requires a somewhat longer and more devoted course of observation than any other is undoubted; but that it has a reward in a greater effect produced, and more delight in the searching, is, the writer thinks, equally certain. We shall find a greater pleasure in proportion to our closer communion with nature, and by a more exact adherence to all her details (for nature has no peculiarities or eccentricities), in whatsoever direction her study may conduct.

This patient devotedness appears to be a conviction peculiar to, or at least more purely followed by, the early Italian painters; a feeling which, exaggerated, and its object mistaken by them, though still held holy and pure, was the cause of the retirement of many of the greatest men from the world to the monastery; there, in undisturbed silence and humility,

> Monotonous to paint
> Those endless cloisters and eternal aisles
> With the same series, Virgin, Babe, and Saint,
> With the same cold, calm, beautiful regard.

Even with this there is not associated a melancholy feeling alone; for, although the object was mistaken, yet there is evinced a consciousness of purpose definite and most elevated; and again, we must remember, as a great cause of this effect, that the Arts were, for the most part, cleric, and not laic, or at least were under the predominant influence of the clergy, who were the most important patrons by far, and their houses the safest receptacles for the works of the great painter.

The modern artist does not retire to monasteries, or practise discipline; but he may show his participation in the same high feeling by a firm attachment to truth in every point of representation, which is the most just method. For how can good be sought by evil means, or by falsehood, or by slight in any degree? By a determination to represent the thing and the whole of the thing, by training himself to the deepest observation of its fact and detail, enabling himself to reproduce, as far as is possible, nature herself, the painter will best evince his share of faith. . . .

It has been said that there is presumption in this movement of the modern school, a want of deference to established authorities, a removing of ancient landmarks. This is best answered by the profession that nothing can be more humble than the pretension to the observation of facts alone, and the truthful rendering of them. If we are not to depart from established principles, how are we to advance at all? Are we to remain still? Remember, no thing remains still; that which does not advance falls backward. That this movement is an advance, and that it is of nature herself, is shown by its going nearer to truth in every object produced, and by its being guided by the very principles the ancient painters followed, as soon as they attained the mere power of representing an object faithfully. These principles are now revived, not from them, though through their example, but from nature herself.

That the earlier painters came nearer to fact, that they were less of the art, artificial, cannot be better shown than by the statement of a few examples from their works. There is a magnificent Niello work by an unknown Florentine artist, on which is a group of the Saviour in the lap of the Virgin. She is old, (a most touching point); lamenting aloud, clutches passionately the heavy-weighted body on her knee; her mouth is open. Altogether it is one of the most powerful appeals possible to be conceived; for there are few but will consider this identification with humanity to be of more effect than any refined or emasculate treatment of the same subject by later artists, in which we have the fact forgotten for the sake of the type of religion, which the Virgin was always taken to represent, whence she is shown as still young; as if, nature being taken typically, it were not better to adhere to the emblem throughout, confident by this means to maintain its appropriateness, and, therefore, its value and force.

[*After three more paragraphs of comment on truth to nature in early Italian art Stephens reinforces his thesis by an argument particularly topical in* 1850: *Sir Charles Lyell's* "*Principles of Geology*" *had appeared in* 1830–33, *and the important* "*Vestiges of the Natural History of Creation*" *anonymously in* 1844.]

The sciences have become almost exact within the present century. Geology and chemistry are almost re-instituted. The first has been nearly created; the second expanded so widely that it now searches and measures the creation. And how has this been done but by bringing greater knowledge to bear upon a wider range of experiment; by being precise in the search after truth? If this adherence to fact, to experiment and not theory—to begin at the beginning and not fly to the end—has added so much to the knowledge of man in science; why may it not greatly assist the moral purposes of the Arts? It cannot be well to degrade a lesson by falsehood. Truth in every particular ought to be the aim of the artist. Admit no untruth: let the priest's garment be clean.

Let us now return to the Early Italian painters. A complete refutation of any charge that the character of their school was necessarily gloomy will be found in the works of Benozzo Gozzoli, as in his *Vineyard*, where there are some grape-gatherers the most elegant and graceful imaginable; this painter's children are the most natural ever painted. In Ghiberti—in Fra Angelico (well named)—in Masaccio, in Ghirlandajo, and in Baccio della Porta, in fact in nearly all the works of the painters of this school, will be found a character of gentleness, grace, and freedom, which cannot be surpassed by any other school, be that which it may; and it is evident that this result must have been obtained by their peculiar attachment to simple nature alone, their casting aside all ornament, or rather their perfect ignorance of such—a happy fortune none have shared with them. To show that with all these qualifications they have been pre-eminent in energy and dignity, let us instance the *Air Demons* of Orcagna, where there is a woman borne through the air by an Evil Spirit. Her expression is the most terrible imaginable; she grasps her bearer with desperation, looking out around her into space, agonized with terror. There are other figures in the same picture of men who have been cast down, and are falling through the air: one descends with his hands tied, his chin up, and long hair hanging from his head in a mass. One of the Evil Spirits hovering over them has flat wings, as though they were made of plank: this gives a most powerful character to the figure. Altogether, this picture contains perhaps a greater amount of bold imagination and originality of conception than any of the kind ever painted. For sublimity there are few works which equal the *Archangels* of Giotto, who stand singly, holding their sceptres, and with relapsed wings. The *Paul* of Masaccio is a well-known example of the dignified simplicity of which these artists possessed so large a share.

[*Repeating that the artist should" be content to study nature alone, and not dream of elevating any of her works," Stephens develops in his next paragraph the idea that " The Arts have always been most important moral guides." He then moves to this peroration.*]

If we have entered upon a new age, a new cycle of man, of which there are many signs, let us have it unstained by this vice of sensuality of mind. The English school has lately lost a great deal of this character; why should we not be altogether free from it? Nothing can degrade a man or a nation more than this meanness; why should we not avoid it? Sensuality is a meanness repugnant to youth, and disgusting in age: a degradation at all times. Let us say:

> My strength is as the strength of ten,
> Because my heart is pure.

Bearing this in mind—the conviction that, without the pure heart, nothing can be done worthy of us; by this, that the most successful school of painters has produced upon us the intention of their earnestness at this distance of time—let us follow in their path, guided by their light: not so subservient as to lose our own freedom, but in the confidence of equal power and equal destiny; and then rely that we shall obtain the same success and equal or greater power, such as is given to the age in which we live. This is the only course that is worthy of the influence which might be exerted by means of the Arts upon the character of the people: therefore let it be the only one for us to follow if we hope to share in the work.

That the real power of the Arts, in conjunction with Poetry, upon the actions of any age is, or might be, predominant above all others will be readily allowed by all that have given any thought to the subject: and that there is no assignable limit to the good that may be wrought by their influence is another point upon which there can be small doubt. Let us then endeavour to call up and exert this power in the worthiest manner, not forgetting that we chose a difficult path in which there are many snares, and holding in mind the motto, *No Cross, no Crown*.

Believe that there is that in the fact of truth, though it be only in the character of a single leaf earnestly studied, which may do its share in the great labour of the world: remember that it is by truth alone that the Arts can ever hold the position for which they were intended, as the most powerful instruments, the most gentle guides; that, of all classes, there is none to whom the celebrated words of Lessing, "That the destinies of a nation depend upon its young men between nineteen and twenty-five years of age," can apply so well as to yourselves. Recollect, that your portion in this is most important: that your share is with the poet's share; that, in every careless thought or neglected doubt, you shelve your duty, and forsake your trust; fulfil and maintain these, whether in the hope of personal fame and fortune, or from a sense of power used to its intentions; and you may hold out both hands to the world.

Trust it, and it will have faith in you; will hearken to the precepts you may have permission to impart.

W. M. ROSSETTI

SONNET FOR "THE GERM"

When whoso merely hath a little thought
  Will plainly think the thought which is in him—
  Not imaging another's bright or dim,
Not mangling with new words what others taught;
When whoso speaks, from having either sought
  Or only found—will speak, not just to skim
  A shallow surface with words made and trim,
But in that very speech the matter brought:
Be not too keen to cry—"So this is all!—
  A thing I might myself have thought as well,
  But would not say it, for it was not worth!"
Ask: "Is this truth?" For is it still to tell
  That, be the theme a point or the whole earth,
Truth is a circle, perfect, great or small?

FORD MADOX BROWN

DESCRIPTIVE COMMENTARY ON "WORK"

THIS picture was begun in 1852 at Hampstead. The background, which represents the main street of that suburb not far from the Heath, was painted on the spot.

At that time extensive excavations were going on in the neighbourhood, and, seeing and studying daily as I did the British excavator, or *navvy*, as he designates himself, in the full swing of his activity (with his manly and picturesque costume, and with the rich glow of colour which exercise under a hot sun will impart), it appeared to me that he was at least as worthy of the powers of an English painter as the fisherman of the Adriatic, the peasant of the Campagna, or the Neapolitan *lazzarone*. Gradually this idea developed itself into that of *Work* as it now exists, with the British excavator for a central group, as the outward and visible type of *Work*. Here are presented the young navvy in the pride of manly health and beauty; the strong fully developed navvy who does his work and loves his beer; the selfish old bachelor navvy, stout of limb, and perhaps a trifle tough in those regions where compassion is said to reside; the navvy of strong animal nature who, but that he was when young *taught* to work at useful work, might even now be working at the *useless crank*. Then Paddy with his larry and his pipe in his mouth. The young navvy who occupies the place of hero in this group, and in the picture, stands on what is termed a landing-stage, a platform placed half-way down the trench; two men from beneath shovel the earth up to him as he shovels it on to the pile outside. Next in value of significance to these is the ragged wretch who has never been *taught to work*; with his restless, gleaming eyes he doubts and despairs of everyone. But for a certain effeminate gentleness of disposition and a love of nature he might have been a burglar! He lives in Flower and Dean Street, where the policemen walk two and two, and the worst cut-throats surround him, but he is harmless; and before the dawn you may see him miles out in the country, collecting his wild weeds and singular plants to awaken interest, and perhaps find a purchaser in some sprouting botanist. When exhausted he will return to his den, his creel of flowers then rests in an open courtyard, the thoroughfare for the crowded inmates of this haunt of vice, and played in by mischievous boys, yet the basket rarely gets interfered with, unless through the unconscious lurch of some drunkard. The breadwinning implements are sacred with the very poor. In the very opposite scale from the man who can't work, at the very further corner of the picture, are two men who appear as having nothing to do. These are the brain-workers, who, seeming to be idle, work, and are the cause of well-ordained work and happiness in others—sages, such as in ancient Greece published their opinions in the market square. Perhaps one of these may already, before he or others know it, have moulded a nation to his pattern, converted a hitherto combative race to obstinate passivity; with a word may have centupled the tide of emigration, with another, have quenched the political passions of both factions—may have reversed men's notions upon criminals, upon slavery, upon many things, and still be walking about little known to some. The other, in friendly communion with the philosopher, smiling perhaps at some of his wild sallies and cynical thrusts (for Socrates at times strangely disturbs the seriousness of his auditory by the mercilessness of his jokes—against vice and foolishness), is intended for a kindred and yet very dissimilar spirit. A clergyman, such as the Church of England offers examples of—a priest without guile—a gentleman without pride, much in communion with the working classes, 'honouring all men,' 'never weary in well-doing.' Scholar, author, philosopher, and teacher, too, in his way, but not above practical efforts, if even for a small resulting good. Deeply penetrated as he is with the axiom that each unit of humanity feels as much as all the rest combined, and impulsive and hopeful in nature, so that the remedy suggests itself to him concurrently with the evil.

Next to these, on the shaded bank, are different characters out of work: haymakers in quest of employment; a Stoic from the Emerald Island, with hay stuffed in his hat to keep the draught out, and need for Stoicism just at present, being short of baccy; a young shoeless Irishman with his wife, feeding their first-born with cold pap; an old sailor turned haymaker; and two young peasants in search of harvest work, reduced in strength, perhaps by fever—possibly by famine. Behind the Pariah, who never has learned to work, appears a group of a very different class, who, from an opposite cause, have not been sufficiently used to work either. These are the *rich*, who 'have no need to work'—not at least for bread—*the 'bread of life'* is neither here nor there. The pastrycook's tray, the symbol of superfluity, accompanies these. It is peculiarly English; I never saw it abroad that I remember, though something of the kind must be used. For some years after returning to England I could never quite get over a certain socialistic twinge on seeing it pass, unreasonable as the feeling may have been. Past the pastrycook's tray come two married ladies. The elder and more serious of the two devotes her energies to tract distributing, and has just flung one entitled 'The Hodman's Haven; or, Drink for Thirsty Souls,' to the somewhat uncompromising specimen of navvy humanity descending the ladder: he scorns it, but with good-nature. This well-intentioned lady has, perhaps, never reflected that excavators may have notions to the effect that ladies might be benefited by receiving tracts containing navvies' ideas! Nor yet that excavators are skilled workmen, shrewd thinkers chiefly, and, in general, men of great experience in life, as life presents itself to them.

In front of her is the lady whose only business in life as yet is to dress and look beautiful for our benefit. She probably possesses everything that can give enjoyment to life; how then can she but enjoy the passing moment, and, like a flower, feed on the light of the sun? Would anyone wish it otherwise? Certainly not I, dear lady. Only in your own interest, seeing that certain benefits cannot be insured for ever—as, for instance, health may fail, beauty fade, pleasures through repetition pall—I will not hint at the greater calamities to which flesh is heir—seeing all this, were you less engaged watching that exceedingly beautiful tiny greyhound in a red jacket that *will* run through that lime, I would beg to call your attention to my group of small, exceedingly ragged, dirty children in the foreground of my picture, where you are about to pass. I would, if permitted, observe that, though at first they may appear just such a group of ragged dirty brats as anywhere get in the way and make a noise, yet, being considered attentively, they, like insects, molluscs, miniature plants, etc., develop qualities to form a most interesting study, and occupy the mind at times when all else might fail to attract. That they are motherless, the baby's black ribbons and their extreme dilapidation indicate, making them all the more worthy of consideration; a mother, however destitute, would scarcely leave the eldest one in such a plight. As to the father, I have no doubt he drinks, and will be sentenced in the police-court for neglecting them. The eldest girl, not more than ten, poor child! is very worn-looking and thin; her frock, evidently the compassionate gift of some grown-up person, she has neither the art nor the means to adapt to her own diminutive proportions—she is fearfully untidy, therefore, and her way of wrenching her brother's hair looks vixenish and against her. But then a germ or rudiment of good housewifery seems to pierce through her disordered envelope, for the younger ones are taken care of, and nestle to her as to a mother; the sun-burnt baby, which looks wonderfully solemn and intellectual, as all babies do, as I have no doubt your own little cherub looks at this moment asleep in its charming bassinet, is fat and well-to-do, it has even been put into poor mourning for its mother. The other little one, though it sucks a piece of carrot in lieu of a sugar-plum, and is shoeless, seems healthy and happy, watching the workmen, The care of the two little ones is an anxious charge for the elder girl, and she has become a premature scold all through having to manage that *boy*—that boy, though a merry, good-natured-looking young Bohemian, is evidently the plague of her life, as boys always are. Even now he *will* not leave that workman's barrow alone, and gets his hair well pulled, as is natural. The dog which accompanies them is evidently of the same outcast sort as themselves. The having to do battle for his existence in a hard world has soured his temper, and he frequently fights, as by his torn ear you may know; but the poor children may do as they like with him; rugged democrat as he is, he is gentle to them, only he hates minions of aristocracy in red jackets. The old bachelor navvy's small valuable bull-pup also instinctively distrusts outlandish-looking dogs in jackets.

The couple on horseback in the middle distance consists of a gentleman, still young, and his daughter. (The rich and the poor both marry early, only those of moderate incomes pro-crastinate). This gentleman is evidently very rich, probably a colonel in the army, with a seat in Parliament, and fifteen thousand a year and a pack of hounds. He is not an over-dressed man of the tailor's dummy sort—he does not put his fortune on his back, he is too rich for that; moreover he looks to me an honest, true-hearted gentleman (he was painted from one I know), and could he only be got to hear what the two sages in the corner have to say, I have no doubt he would be easily won over. But the road is blocked, and the daughter says we must go back, papa, round the other way.

The man with the beer-tray, calling "Beer ho!" so lustily, is a specimen of town pluck and energy contrasted with country thews and sinews. He is hump-backed, stunted in his growth, and in all matters of taste vulgar as Birmingham can make him look in the nineteenth century. As a child he was probably starved, stunted with gin, and suffered to get run over. But energy has brought him through to be a prosperous beer-man, and 'very much respected,' and in his way he also is a sort of hero; that black eye was got probably doing the police of his master's establishment, and in an encounter with some huge ruffian whom he has conquered in fight, and hurled out through the swing-doors of the palace of gin prone on to the pavement. On the walls are posters and bills, one of the "Boy's Home, 41, Euston Road," which the lady who is giving tracts will no doubt subscribe to presently, and place the urchin playing with the barrow in; one of "The Working Men's College, Great Ormond Street," or if you object to these, then a police bill offering 50*l.* reward in a matter of highway robbery. Back in the distance we see the Assembly-room of the "Flamstead Institute of Arts," where Professor Snoöx is about to repeat his interesting lecture on the habits of the domestic cat. Indignant pussies up on the roof are denying his theory *in toto*.

The less important characters in the background require little comment. Bobus, our old friend, "the sausage-maker of Houndsditch," from *Past and Present*, having secured a colossal fortune (he boasts of it *now*) by anticipating the French Hippophage Society in the introduction of horseflesh as a *cheap* article of human food, is at present going in for the county of Middlesex, and, true to his old tactics, has hired all the idlers in the neighbourhood to carry his boards. These being one too many for the bearers, an old woman has volunteered to carry the one in excess.

The episode of the policeman who has caught an orange-girl in the heinous offence of resting her basket on a post, and who himself administers justice in the shape of a push that sends her fruit all over the road, is one of common occurrence —or used to be—perhaps the police now 'never do such things.'

I am sorry to say that most of my friends, on examining this part of my picture, have laughed over it as a good joke. Only two men saw the circumstance in a different light; one of them was the young Irishman who feeds his infant with pap. Pointing to it with his thumb, his mouth quivering at the reminiscence, he said, "That, Sir, *I* know to be true." The other was a clergyman; his testimony would perhaps have more weight. I dedicate this portion of the work to the Commissioner of Police.

Through this picture I have gained some experience of the navvy class, and I have usually found, that if you can break through the upper crust of *mauvaise honte* which surrounds them in common with most Englishmen, and which, in the case of the navvies, I believe to be the cause of much of their bad language, you will find them serious, intelligent men, and with much to interest in their conversation, which, moreover, contains about the same amount of morality and sentiment that is commonly found among men in the active and hazardous walks of life, for that their career is one of hazard and danger none should doubt. Many stories might be told of navvies' daring and endurance, were this the place for them. One incident peculiarly connected with this picture is the melancholy fact that one of the very men who sat for it lost his life by a scaffold accident before I had yet quite done with him. I remember the poor fellow telling me, among other things, how he never but once felt nervous with his work, and this was having to trundle barrows of earth over a plank-line crossing a rapid river at a height of *eighty feet* above the water. But it was not the height he complained of, it was the *gliding motion of the water underneath*.

I have only to observe, in conclusion, that the effect of hot July sunlight, attempted in this picture, has been introduced because it seems peculiarly fitted to display *work* in all its severity, and not from any predilection for this kind of light over any other.

N.B. In several cases I have had the advantage of sittings from personages of note, who, at a loss of time to themselves, have kindly contributed towards the greater truthfulness of some of the characters. As my object, however, in all cases, is to delineate types and not individuals, and as, moreover, I never contemplated employing their renown to benefit my own reputation, I refrain from publishing their names.

WILLIAM MORRIS

THE AIMS OF ART

[*Only the centre section of this stimulating essay, too long to quote in its entirety, is reproduced. Morris's premise has been that the primary aim of art is to give pleasure " or, shortly, to make man's work happy and his rest fruitful." He continues:*]

CONSEQUENTLY, genuine art is an unmixed blessing to the race of man.

But as the word 'genuine' is a large qualification, I must ask leave to attempt to draw some practical conclusions from this assertion of the Aims of Art, which will, I suppose, or indeed hope, lead us into some controversy on the subject; because it is futile indeed to expect anyone to speak about art, except in the most superficial way, without encountering those social problems which all serious men are thinking of; since art is and must be, either in its abundance or its barrenness, in its sincerity or its hollowness, the expression of the society amongst which it exists.

First, then, it is clear to me that, at the present time, those who look widest at things and deepest into them are quite dissatisfied with the present state of the arts, as they are also with the present condition of society. This I say in the teeth of the supposed revivification of art which has taken place of late years: in fact, that very excitement about the arts amongst a part of the cultivated people of today does but show on how firm a basis the dissatisfaction above mentioned rests. Forty years ago there was much less talk about art, much less practice of it than there is now; and that is specially true of the architectural arts, which I shall mostly have to speak about now. People have consciously striven to raise the dead in art since that time, and with some superficial success. Nevertheless, in spite of this conscious effort, I must tell you that England, to a person who can feel and understand beauty, was a less grievous place to live in then than it is now; and we who feel what art means know well, though we do not often dare to say so, that forty years hence it will be a more grievous place to us than it is now if we still follow up the road we are on. Less than forty years ago—about thirty—I first saw the city of Rouen, then still in its outward aspect a piece of the Middle Ages; no words can tell you how its mingled beauty, history, and romance took hold on me; I can only say that, looking back on my past life, I find it was the greatest pleasure I have ever had: and now it is a pleasure which no one can ever have again: it is lost to the world for ever. At that time I was an undergraduate of Oxford. Though not so astounding, so romantic, or at first sight so medieval as the Norman city, Oxford in those days still kept a great deal of its earlier loveliness: and the memory of its grey streets as they then were has been an abiding influence and pleasure in my life, and would be greater still if I could only forget what they are now—a matter of far more importance than the so-called learning of the place could have been to me in any case, but which, as it was, no one tried to teach me, and I did not try to learn. Since then the guardians of this beauty and romance so fertile of education, though professedly engaged in "the higher education" (as the futile system of compromises which they follow is nick-named), have ignored it utterly, have made its preservation give way to the pressure of commercial exigencies, and are determined apparently to destroy it altogether. There is another pleasure for the world gone down the wind; here, again, the beauty and romance have been uselessly, causelessly, most foolishly thrown away.

These two cases are given simply because they have been fixed in my mind; they are but types of what is going on everywhere throughout civilization: the world is everywhere growing uglier and more commonplace, in spite of the conscious and very strenuous efforts of a small group of people towards the revival of art, which are so obviously out of joint with the tendency of the age that, while the uncultivated have not even heard of them, the mass of the cultivated look upon them as a joke, and even that they are now beginning to get tired of.

Now, if it be true, as I have asserted, that genuine art is an unmixed blessing to the world, this is a serious matter; for at first sight it seems to show that there will soon be no art at all in the world, which will thus lose an unmixed blessing; it can ill afford to do that, I think.

For art, if it has to die, has worn itself out, and its aim will be a thing forgotten; and its aim was to make work happy and rest fruitful. Is all work to be unhappy, all rest unfruitful, then? Indeed, if art is to perish, that will be the case, unless something is to take its place—something at present unnamed, undreamed of.

I do not think that anything will take the place of art; not that I doubt the ingenuity of man, which seems to be boundless in the direction of making himself unhappy, but because I believe the springs of art in the human mind to be deathless, and also because it seems to me easy to see the causes of the present obliteration of the arts.

For we civilized people have not given them up consciously, or of our free will; we have been *forced* to give them up. Perhaps I can illustrate that by the detail of the application of machinery to the production of things in which artistic form of some sort is possible. Why does a reasonable man use a machine? Surely to save his labour. There are some things which a machine can do as well as a man's hand, *plus* a tool, can do them. He need not, for instance, grind his corn in a hand quern; a little trickle of water, a wheel, and a few simple contrivances will do it all perfectly well, and leave him free to smoke his pipe and think, or to carve the handle of his knife. That, so far, is unmixed gain in the use of a machine—always, mind you, supposing equality of condition among men; no art is lost, leisure or time for more pleasurable work is gained. Perhaps a perfectly reasonable and free man would stop there in his dealings with machinery; but such reason and freedom are too much to expect, so let us follow our machine inventor a step farther. He has to weave plain cloth, and finds doing so dullish on the one hand, and on the other that a power-loom will weave the cloth nearly as well as a hand-loom; so, in order to gain more leisure or time for more pleasurable work, he uses a power-loom, and foregoes the small advantage of the little extra art in the cloth. But so doing, as far as the art is concerned, he has not got a pure gain; he has made a bargain between art and labour, and got a makeshift as a consequence. I do not say that he may not be right in so doing, but that he has lost as well as gained. Now, this is as far as a man who values art and is reasonable would go in the matter of machinery *as long as he was free*—that is, was not *forced* to work for another man's profit; so long as he was living in a society *that had accepted equality of condition*. Carry the machine used for art a step farther, and he becomes an unreasonable man, if he values art and is free. To avoid misunderstanding I must say that I am thinking of the modern machine, which is as it were alive, as to which the man is auxiliary, and not of the old machine, the improved tool, which is auxiliary to the man, and only works as long as his hand is thinking; though I will remark, that even this elementary form of machine has to be dropped when we come to the higher and more intricate forms of art. Well, as to the machine proper used for art, when it gets to the stage above dealing with a necessary production that has accidentally some beauty about it, a reasonable man with a feeling for art will only use it when he is *forced* to. If he thinks he would like ornament, for instance, and knows that the machine cannot do it properly, and does not care to spend the time to do it properly, why should he do it at all? He will not diminish his leisure for the sake of making something he does not want unless some man or band of men force him to do it; so he will either go without the ornament, or sacrifice some of his leisure to have it genuine. That will be a sign that he wants it very much, and that it will be worth his trouble: in which case, again, his labour on it will not be mere trouble, but will interest and please him by satisfying the needs of his mood of energy.

This, I say, is how a reasonable man would act if he were free from man's compulsion; not being free, he acts very differently. He has long passed the stage at which machines are only used for doing work repulsive to an average man, or for doing what could be as well done by a machine as a man, and he instinctively expects a machine to be invented whenever any product of industry becomes sought after. He is the slave to machinery; the new machine *must* be invented, and when invented he *must*—I will not say use it, but be used by it, whether he likes it or not.

But why is he the slave to machinery? Because he is the slave to the system for whose existence the invention of machinery was necessary.

And now I must drop, or rather have dropped, the assumption of equality of condition, and remind you that, though in a sense we are all the slaves of machinery, yet that some men are so directly without any metaphor at all, and that these are just those on whom the great body of the arts depends—the workmen. It is necessary for the system which keeps them in their position as an inferior class that they should either be themselves machines or be the servants to machines, in no case having any interest in the work which they turn out. To their employers they are, so far as they are workmen, a part of the machinery of the workshop or the factory; to themselves they are proletarians, human beings working to live that they may live to work; their part of craftsmen, of makers of things by their own free will, is played out.

At the risk of being accused of sentimentality, I will say that since this is so, since the work which produces the things that should be matters of art is but a burden and a slavery, I exult in this at least, that it cannot produce art; that all it can do lies between stark utilitarianism and idiotic sham.

Or indeed is that merely sentimental? Rather, I think, we who have learned to see the connection between industrial slavery and the degradation of the arts have learned also to hope for a future for those arts; since the day will certainly come when men will shake off the yoke, and refuse to accept the mere artificial compulsion of the gambling market to waste their lives in ceaseless and hopeless toil, and when it does come, their instincts for beauty and imagination set free along with them, will produce such art as they need; and who can say that it will not as far surpass the art of past ages as that does the poor relics of it left us by the age of commerce?

A word or two on an objection which has often been made to me when I have been talking on this subject. It may be said, and is often, You regret the art of the Middle Ages (as indeed I do), but those who produced it were not free, they were serfs, or gild-craftsmen surrounded by brazen walls of trade restrictions; they had no political rights, and were exploited by their masters, the noble caste, most grievously. Well, I quite admit that the oppression and violence of the Middle Ages had its effect on the art of those days, its short-comings are traceable to them; they repressed art in certain directions, I do not doubt that; and for that reason I say, that when we shake off the present oppression as we shook off the old, we may expect the art of the days of real freedom to rise above that of those old violent days. But I do say that it was possible then to have social, organic, hopeful progressive art; whereas now such poor scraps of it as are left are the result of individual and wasteful struggle, are retrospective and pessi-mistic. And this hopeful art was possible amidst all the oppression of those days, because the instruments of that oppression were grossly obvious, and were external to the work of the craftsman. They were laws and customs obviously intended to rob him, and open violence of the highway-robbery kind. In short, industrial production was not the instrument used for robbing the "lower classes"; it is now the main instrument used in that honourable profession. The medieval craftsman was free on his work, therefore he made it as amusing to himself as he could; and it was his pleasure and not his pain that made all things beautiful that were made, and lavished treasures of human hope and thought on everything that man made, from a cathedral to a porridge-pot. Come, let us put it in the way least respectful to the medieval craftsman, most polite to the modern 'hand': the poor devil of the fourteenth century, his work was of so little value that he was allowed to waste it by the hour in pleasing himself—and others; but our highly-strung mechanic, his minutes are too rich with the burden of perpetual profit for him to be allowed to waste one of them on art; the present system will not allow him—cannot allow him—to produce works of art.

W. HOLMAN HUNT

From the Conclusion to

"PRE-RAPHAELITISM AND THE PRE-RAPHAELITE BROTHERHOOD"

[*At the end of Vol. II, Chapter XVI, Hunt, surveying the aims and achievements of the P.R.B., is substantiating his claim that "All art from the beginning served for the higher development of men's minds."*]

IT has been seen how in a quite child-like way we at the beginning set ourselves to illustrate themes which we conscientiously persuaded ourselves to be connected with the pathetic, the honest, the laudable, the sublime interests of humanity. When we treated of vicious power triumphant, it was to excite honest pity for the victims, and indignation towards arrogant vice. Some honest men that I have met have asked me with unaffected concern whether artists paint their subjects with full conviction, or merely as a bid for popular favour. Sincerity or insincerity of artists must of necessity reveal itself in their works. Take Millais as a fair exponent of our purpose; he only exceptionally painted so-called religious subjects, but he loved to illustrate what may justly be looked upon as holy themes. The story of Lorenzo and Isabella, considered on moral grounds, is thoroughly healthy and sound in its claim to human sympathy and interest; their affections were obnoxious to no righteous judgment, but only inimical to false pride and vanity. In his picture *L'Enfant du Regiment*, the child sleeping on the warrior's tomb, contrasted with surrounding violence and bloodshed, typified the trustful peace which the building was originally destined to give. Although the work is not labelled religious, it may be regarded as a Christian homily. His *Blind Girl*, moreover, is a heart-felt appeal to commiseration. *The Rescuing Fireman* provokes expansive recognition of the Divine in unpretentious humanity. Rossetti's early designs were pronouncedly religious, and his design of *Found* was, in the just sense, intrinsically so. These pictures by my two companions would be enough to prove that our purpose had not only a newness in its outer form, but also took up in more extended aspiration the principle exemplifying that "Art is Love." . . .

Before pronouncing the last words of this book, it is needful to declare that, notwithstanding what may seem to some inconsistent digressions, it is a history of a movement which strove to bring greater healthiness and integrity to every branch of formative art; architecture, sculpture, decorative design, and imitative painting, which are all dependent upon the use of materials for expression. In the effort to purge our art of what was in the nature of bathos, affected in sentiment and unworthy according to wholesome English tradition, we were following the example of the poets of the early Victorian age. All manly in their vindications of virtue, although some spoke in an over-feminine tone, our exemplars in letters had all been in accord to prune English imagination of unwholesome foreign precedent, tawdry glitter, and theatrical pomposity, corruptions which had descended from the attitudinisers of the two earlier reigns. The literary reformers, still declaiming in our day, had already revived the robust interest in humanity exercised by British men of genius in past centuries.

[*In his next, and final, chapter this nationalist approach to art takes the form of an attack on the "insidious corruption" of study in foreign art schools. Then, after analysing Titian's "Bacchus and Ariadne" to prove his ability to recognize as great a picture with no overt moral purpose, Hunt ends the book by defining the main dangers threatening art at the end of the century.*]

I must speak here more emphatically against servile medievalism. Students should never be enticed to meander among the graves, piping resurrected strains, sweet though they may be, forgetful of their own life-battle. . . .

The nineteenth century will be known as an age of 'revivals.' Literary medieval resuscitations began first perhaps in England, but accentuated feminine development of the Italian Renaissance in graphic art came to us through a narrow section of the Germans. The gratitude of the world for the excellence of the productions of the past transiently endowed their modern imitations with a sweeter taste than unripened works with a new flavour are at first found to possess. The imitator's task being a pleasant and easy one, the resemblance of the work to its prototype gains for it a more impetuous welcome than is accorded to the less mature achievements of original inspiration. These last, unfamiliar to the eye, are precluded by their strangeness from immediate reception. There is scarcely danger of shipwreck on the well-sounded waters of a tidal service, while there is frequent peril to a ship on an unknown sea. It has seemed to me right to warn the world against what may be called *servility* to antiquity, but our present danger is a cry of opposite tenor, that artists should begin their practice without the equipment which the teaching of their great precursors gives. He is only a quack who commences ministering to the sick in ignorance of those carefully tested experiments which have led to modern methods of healing, for while the traditions of the ancients must not be accepted as binding, all that they said and did demands thought from the attentive

THE LADY OF SHALOTT

W. Holman Hunt

physician, an equal docility is called for from beginners in art. To be ignorant of the stages by which the great masters arrived at their pre-eminence, and to be indifferent to the studied training of the eye and hand which they underwent, is a besotted course.

Present exhibitions of painting and sculpture, so full of productions that show disregard or defiance of the fundamental principles of sanity and reverence, supply proof that quackery is in highest favour; and the timid spectator (dismayed at the abominations) is told by the adorers of such uncultivated out-pourings that not to admire is to be a Philistine; that the chaotic mass called a work of art is really the product of the most modern, and therefore the most advanced thought. . . .

Instead of adorable pictures of nature's face, we are offered representations of scenes that none but those with blunted feelings could contemplate, not stopping short of the interiors of slaughter-houses. The degradation of art is nothing less than a sign of disease in Society.

But enough of this humiliating topic! I must return to the defence of the Pre-Raphaelites. After fifty or sixty years, with full count of our disappointments as of our successes, it may be confidently affirmed that the principle of our reform in art was a sound one. With some remarkable exceptions, art in our youth had become puerile and doting, and it was high time to find a remedy. It stirred us to proclaim that art should interpret to men how much more beautiful the world is, not only in every natural form, but in every pure principle of human life, than they would without her aid deem it to be. If artists' work misguides men, making them believe that there is no order in creation, no wisdom in evolution, decrying the sublime influences as purposeless, we shall indeed be a sorry brood of men. . . .

[*Hunt now digresses on the inordinate influence upon the reputation of artists wielded by professional art critics, most of whom are deficient in technical and practical knowledge.*]

Hazlitt and Ruskin . . . were, with all their eccentricities, elucidating critics, because they themselves in certain branches were practised artists, Ruskin being the most perfect in that to which he especially devoted himself in criticism. But the writers who became the mouthpieces of the cabal that sought to ruin Pre-Raphaelitism had scarcely even drawn a line, and they came to their task without understanding humility or restraint. It is devoutly to be hoped that writers determining the fate of future art will think seriously of the havoc wrought in the past, and of their own eternal responsibility for the judgment they exercise.

In conclusion let me warn the world that the threat to modern art, menacing nothing less than its extinction, lies in "Impressionism" as a dogma without any regard to its limitations. The word "Impressionism," as used for the main ambition of art, is mere cant, offensive to all who really have acquaintance with the profound subtleties of art practice, yet by blatant repetition and determined assurance trumpeted by idle writers, multitudes are cowed into silence, and become incapable of expressing the opinion which common-sense suggests to them as to the vacuous nature of such pretensions as the 'modernity' of today reveals. The few better-educated artists who, perhaps by fellow-studentship, have been entrapped to figure as monarchs of a draggled herd do sometimes lend a redeeming grace to the pretensions of the school; but I must, in treating this subject, declare that as a rule the greater part of the work figuring under the name of "Impressionism" is childishly drawn and modelled, ignorantly coloured and handled, materialistic and soulless. . . .

For the consideration of those who come after us, ere I give up my record of our Pre-Raphaelite purpose, I must reiterate that our determination in our reform was to abjure alliance with re-classicalism, to avoid revived quattro- or cinque-centism, already powerfully represented in England, and to supplant the cramped dogmas founded on these fashions by devoting our allegiance to Nature, and to magnifying her teachings for further inspiration. We never refused admiration to Raphael nor to his still more prodigious elder contemporaries, Michael Angelo and Leonardo da Vinci, neither did we refuse whatever vital teaching there was in any ancient master or school. We may not in our youth have seen the extent of Reynolds's power; for it needed a more advanced experience to give full knowledge of the variety and richness of his harnessed genius. In principle, however, I maintain that we had justice on our side in thinking that his homage to the founders of Academies, such as the Caracci and Le Brun, led him to prescribe laws derived from them, which crippled the future development of art. . . .

Let it be added that the triumvirate of art in Italy and the company of great English painters who founded the British School were too kingly and too daring in judgment, in their own work too strong in humility towards nature, to be bound by the rules which they of necessity prescribed for their pupils. The famous dictum of Sir Joshua that "rules were not the fetters of genius, but only of those who have no genius," we determined to construe with a more radical rendering than his pupils first gave it, for we decided that the result of its narrow interpretation by his followers had been paralysing, and that henceforth it should form no shackles to future investigation of truth. Had his remarks been limited to the observance of the sciences which form the base of graphic representation, such as the undeviating laws of perspective and the forms and proportions of human and animal creation, his dictum could never have been gainsaid, but Reynolds's dogma was accepted for the control of imaginative liberty; it was in that sense that we dared to rebel against it. If this scaffolding had been of use at first, it had done its work, and we required that it should be put aside as in no sense belonging to the permanent structure of art. The windows of the edifice should be opened to the purity of the azure sky, the prismatic sweetness of the distant hills, the gaiety of hue in the spreading landscape, and the infinite richness of vegetation. Nothing should henceforth be hidden from the enfranchised eye; we undertook to show that the rendering of new delights was not incompatible with the dignity of the highest art. The purpose of art is, in love of guileless beauty, to lead men to distinguish between that which, being clean in spirit, is productive of virtue, and that which is flaunting and meretricious and productive of ruin to a Nation.

THE BEGGAR MAID

W. Holman Hunt

WILLIAM BELL SCOTT

To The Artists called P.R.B. (1851)

I thank you, brethren in Sincerity—
    One who, within the temperate climes of Art,
    From the charmed circle humbly stands apart,

Scornfully also, with a listless eye
Watching old marionettes' vitality;
   For you have shown, with youth's brave confidence,
   The honesty of true speech and the sense
Uniting life with 'nature,' earth with sky.

In faithful hearts Art strikes its roots far down,
   And bears both flower and fruit with seeded core;
   When truth dies out, the fruit appears no more.
But the flower hides a worm within its crown.
   God-speed you onward! Once again our way
   Shall be made odorous with fresh flowers of May.

PRE-RAPHAELITE CREATIVE WRITING

DANTE GABRIEL ROSSETTI

FROM "HAND AND SOUL"

[*This prose study tells the story of an imaginary young painter of the thirteenth century, Chiaro dell' Erma, who believes himself capable of surpassing the work of the established masters and directs his efforts to that end.*]

. . . He now took to work diligently; not returning to Arezzo, but remaining in Pisa, that no day more might be lost; only living entirely to himself. Sometimes, after nightfall, he would walk abroad in the most solitary places he could find; hardly feeling the ground under him because of the thoughts of the day which held him in fever.

The lodging he had chosen was in a house that looked upon gardens fast by the Church of San Rocco. During the offices, as he sat at work, he could hear the music of the organ, and the long murmur that the chanting left; and if his windows were open, sometimes, at those parts of the mass where there is silence throughout the church, his ear caught faintly the single voice of the priest. Beside the matters of his art and a very few books, almost the only object to be noticed in Chiaro's room was a small consecrated image of St Mary Virgin wrought out of silver, before which stood always, in summer-time, a glass containing a lily and a rose.

It was here, and at this time, that Chiaro painted the Dresden pictures; as also, in all likelihood, the one—inferior in merit, but certainly his—which is now at Munich. For the most part, he was calm and regular in his manner of study; though often he would remain at work through the whole of a day, not resting once so long as the light lasted; flushed, and with the hair from his face. Or, at times, when he could not paint, he would sit for hours in thought of all the greatness the world had known from of old; until he was weak with yearning, like one who gazes upon a path of stars.

[*Chiaro, while achieving a measure of success, cannot create the master-piece of which he believes himself capable. After seeing some of his frescoes ruined in a brawl, he is overwhelmed with a despairing sense of frustration.*]

. . . As Chiaro was in these thoughts, the fever encroached slowly on his veins, till he could sit no longer, and would have risen; but suddenly he found awe within him, and held his head bowed, without stirring. The warmth of the air was not shaken; but there seemed a pulse in the light, and a living fresh-ness, like rain. The silence was a painful music, that made the blood ache in his temples; and he lifted his face and his deep eyes.

A woman was present in his room, clad to the hands and feet with a green and grey raiment, fashioned to that time. It seemed that the first thoughts he had ever known were given him as at first from her eyes, and he knew her hair to be the golden veil through which he beheld his dreams. Though her hands were joined, her face was not lifted, but set forward; and though the gaze was austere, yet her mouth was supreme in gentleness. And as he looked, Chiaro's spirit appeared abashed of its own intimate presence, and his lips shook with the thrill of tears; it seemed such a bitter while till the spirit might be indeed alone.

She did not move closer towards him, but he felt her to be as much with him as his breath. He was like one who, scaling a great steepness, hears his own voice echoed in some place much higher than he can see, and the name of which is not known to him. As the woman stood, her speech was with

Chiaro: not, as it were, from her mouth or in his ears; but distinctly between them.

"I am an image, Chiaro, of thine own soul within thee. See me, and know me as I am. Thou sayest that fame has failed thee, and faith failed thee; but because at least thou hast not laid thy life unto riches, therefore, though thus late, I am suffered to come into thy knowledge. Fame sufficed not, for that thou didst seek fame: seek thine own conscience (not thy mind's conscience, but thine heart's), and all shall approve and suffice. For Fame, in noble soils, is a fruit of the Spring: but not therefore should it be said: 'Lo! my garden that I planted is barren: the crocus is here, but the lily is dead in the dry ground, and shall not lift the earth that covers it: therefore, I will fling my garden together, and give it unto the builders.' Take heed rather that thou trouble not the wise secret earth; for in the mould that thou throwest up shall the first tender growth lie to waste; which else had been made strong in its season. Yea, and even if the year fall past in all its months, and the soil be indeed, to thee, peevish and incapable, and though thou indeed gather all thy harvest, and it suffice for others, and thou remain vext with emptiness; and others drink of thy streams, and the drouth rasp thy throat—let it be enough that these have found the feast good, and thanked the giver: remembering that, when the winter is striven through, there is another year, whose wind is meek, and whose sun fulfilleth all."

While he heard, Chiaro went slowly on his knees. It was not to her that spoke, for the speech seemed within him and his own. The air brooded in sunshine, and though the turmoil was great outside, the air within was at peace. But when he looked in her eyes, he wept. And she came to him, and cast her hair over him, and took her hands about his forehead, and spoke again:

"Thou hast said," she continued, gently, "that faith failed thee. This cannot be so. Either thou hadst it not, or thou hast it. But who bade thee strike the point betwixt love and faith? Wouldst thou sift the warm breeze from the sun that quickens it? Who bade thee turn upon God and say: 'Behold, my offering is of earth, and not worthy: thy fire comes not upon it: therefore, though I slay not my brother whom thou acceptest, I will depart before thou smite me.' Why shouldst thou rise up and tell God He is not content? Had He, of His warrant, certified so to thee? Be not nice to seek out division; but possess thy love in sufficiency: assuredly this is faith, for the heart must believe first. What He hath set in thine heart to do, that do thou; and even though thou do it without thought of Him, it shall be well done: it is this sacrifice that He asketh of thee, and His flame is upon it for a sign. Think not of Him; but of His love and thy love. . . . Know that there is but this means whereby thou may'st serve God with man—set thine hand and thy soul to serve man with God."

And when she that spoke had said these words within Chiaro's spirit, she left his side quietly, and stood up as he had first seen her; with her fingers laid together, and her eyes steadfast, and with the breadth of her long dress covering her feet on the floor. And, speaking again, she said:

"Chiaro, servant of God, take now thine Art unto thee, and paint me thus, as I am, to know me: weak, as I am, and in the weeds of this time; only with eyes which seek out labour, and with a faith, not learned, yet jealous of prayer. Do this; so shall thy soul stand before thee always, and perplex thee no more."

And Chiaro did as she bade him. While he worked, his face grew solemn with knowledge: and before the shadows had turned, his work was done. Having finished, he lay back where he sat, and was asleep immediately: for the growth of that strong sunset was heavy about him, and he felt weak and haggard; like one just come out of a dusk, hollow country, bewildered with echoes, where he had lost himself, and who has not slept for many days and nights. And when she saw him lie back, the beautiful woman came to him, and sat at his head, gazing, and quieted his sleep with her voice.

The tumult of the factions had endured all that day through all Pisa, though Chiaro had not heard it: and the last service of that Feast was a mass sung at midnight from the windows of all the churches for the many dead who lay about the city, and who had to be buried before morning, because of the extreme heats.

. . . .

In the Spring of 1847 I was at Florence. Such as were there at the same time with myself—those, at least, to whom Art is something—will certainly recollect how many rooms of the Pitti Gallery were closed through that season, in order that some of the pictures they contained might be examined, and repaired without the necessity of removal. The hall, the stair-cases, and the vast central suite of apartments, were the only accessible portions; and in these such paintings as they could admit from the sealed *penetralia* were profanely huddled together, without respect of dates, schools, or persons.

I fear that, through this interdict, I may have missed seeing many of the best pictures. I do not mean *only* the most talked of: for these, as they were restored, generally found their way somehow into the open rooms, owing to the clamours raised by the students; and I remember how old Ercoli's, the curator's, spectacles used to be mirrored in the reclaimed surface, as he leaned mysteriously over these works with some of the visitors, to scrutinize and elucidate.

One picture, that I saw that Spring, I shall not easily forget. It was among those, I believe, brought from the other rooms, and had been hung, obviously out of all chronology, immediately beneath that head by Raphael so long known as the "Berrettino," and now said to be the portrait of Cecco Ciulli.

The picture I speak of is a small one, and represents merely the figure of a woman, clad to the hands and feet with a green and grey raiment, chaste, and early in its fashion, but exceedingly simple. She is standing: her hands are held together lightly, and her eyes set earnestly open.

The face and hands in this picture, though wrought with great delicacy, have the appearance of being painted at once, in a single sitting: the drapery is unfinished. As soon as I saw the figure, it drew an awe upon me, like water in shadow. I shall not attempt to describe it more than I have already done; for the most absorbing wonder of it was its literality. You knew that figure, when painted, had been seen; yet it was not a thing to be seen of men. This language will appear ridiculous to such as have never looked on the work; and it may be even to some among those who have. On examining it closely, I perceived in one corner of the canvas the words *Manus Animam pinxit*, and the date 1239.

I turned to my Catalogue, but that was useless, for the pictures were all displaced. I then stepped up to the Cavaliere Ercoli, who was in the room at the moment, and asked him regarding the subject and authorship of the painting. He treated the matter, I thought, somewhat slightingly, and said that he could show me the reference in the Catalogue, which he had compiled. This, when found, was not of much value, as it merely said, "Schizzo d'autore incerto," adding the inscription. I could willingly have prolonged my inquiry, in the hope that it might somehow lead to some result; but I had disturbed the curator from certain yards of Guido, and he was not communicative. I went back therefore, and stood before the picture till it grew dusk.

The next day I was there again; but this time a circle of students was round the spot, all copying the "Berrettino." I contrived, however, to find a place whence I could see *my* picture, and where I seemed to be in nobody's way. For some minutes I remained undisturbed; and then I heard, in an English voice: "Might I beg of you, sir, to stand a little more to this side, as you interrupt my view."

I felt vext, for, standing where he asked me, a glare struck on the picture from the windows, and I could not see it. However, the request was reasonably made, and from a countryman;

so I complied, and turning away, stood by his easel. I knew it was not worth while; yet I referred in some way to the work underneath the one he was copying. He did not laugh, but he smiled as we do in England: "*Very* odd, is it not?" said he.

The other students near us were all continental; and seeing an Englishman select an Englishman to speak with, conceived, I suppose, that he could understand no language but his own. They had evidently been noticing the interest which the little picture appeared to excite in me.

One of them, an Italian, said something to another who stood next to him. He spoke with a Genoese accent, and I lost the sense in the villainous dialect. "Che so?" replied the other, lifting his eyebrows towards the figure; "roba mistica: 'st' Inglesi son matti sul misticismo: somiglia alle nebbie di là. Li fa pensare alla patria,

> E intenerisce il core
> Lo dì ch' han detto ai dolci amici adio."

"La notte, vuoi dire," said a third.

There was a general laugh. My compatriot was evidently a novice in the language, and did not take in what was said. I remained silent, being amused.

"Et toi donc?" said he who had quoted Dante, turning to a student, whose birthplace was unmistakable even had he been addressed in any other language: "Que dis-tu de ce genre-là?"

"Moi?" returned the Frenchman, standing back from his easel, and looking at me and at the figure, quite politely, though with an evident reservation: " Je dis, mon cher, que c'est une spécialité dont je me fiche pas mal. Je tiens que quand on ne comprend pas une chose, c'est qu'elle ne signifie rien."

My reader thinks possibly that the French student was right.

I should here say, that in the catalogue for the year just over, (owing, as in cases before mentioned, to the zeal and enthusiasm of

Dr Aemmster) this, and several other pictures, have been more competently entered. The work in question is now placed in the *Sala Sessagona*, a room I did not see—under the number 161. It is described as "Figura mistica di Chiaro dell' Erma," and there is a brief notice of the author appended.

THE BLESSED DAMOZEL

THE blessed damozel leaned out
   From the gold bar of Heaven;
Her eyes were deeper than the depth
   Of waters stilled at even;
She had three lilies in her hand,
   And the stars in her hair were seven.

Her robe, ungirt from clasp to hem,
   No wrought flowers did adorn,
But a white rose of Mary's gift,
   For service meetly worn;
Her hair that lay along her back
   Was yellow like ripe corn.

Herseemed she scarce had been a day
   One of God's choristers;
The wonder was not yet quite gone
   From that still look of hers;
Albeit, to them she left, her day
   Had counted as ten years.

(To one, it is ten years of years.
   . . . Yet now, and in this place,
Surely she leaned o'er me—her hair
   Fell all about my face. . . .
Nothing: the autumn-fall of leaves.
   The whole year sets apace.)

It was the rampart of God's house
   That she was standing on;
By God built over the sheer depth
   The which is Space begun;
So high, that looking downward thence
   She scarce could see the sun.

It lies in Heaven, across the flood
   Of ether, as a bridge.
Beneath, the tides of day and night
   With flame and darkness ridge
The void, as low as where this earth
   Spins like a fretful midge.

Around her, lovers, newly met
   'Mid deathless love's acclaims,
Spoke evermore among themselves
   Their heart-remembered names;
And the souls mounting up to God.
   Went by her like thin flames.

And still she bowed herself and stooped
   Out of the circling charm;
Until her bosom must have made
   The bar she leaned on warm,
And the lilies lay as if asleep
   Along her bended arm.

From the fixed place of Heaven she saw
   Time like a pulse shake fierce
Through all the worlds. Her gaze still strove
   Within the gulf to pierce
Its path; and now she spoke as when
   The stars sang in their spheres.

The sun was gone now; the curled moon
   Was like a little feather
Fluttering far down the gulf; and now
   She spoke through the still weather.
Her voice was like the voice the stars
   Had when they sang together.

(Ah sweet! Even now, in that bird's song,
   Strove not her accents there,
Fain to be hearkened? When those bells
   Possessed the mid-day air,
Strove not her steps to reach my side
   Down all the echoing stair?)

"I wish that he were come to me,
   For he will come," she said.
"Have I not prayed in Heaven?—on earth,
   Lord, Lord, has he not pray'd?
Are not two prayers a perfect strength?
   And shall I feel afraid?

"When around his head the aureole clings,
   And he is clothed in white,
I'll take his hand and go with him
   To the deep wells of light;
As unto a stream we will step down,
   And bathe there in God's sight.

"We two will stand beside that shrine,
   Occult, withheld, untrod,
Whose lamps are stirred continually
   With prayer sent up to God;
And see our old prayers, granted, melt
   Each like a little cloud.

"We two will lie i' the shadow of
     That living mystic tree
Within whose secret growth the Dove
     Is sometimes felt to be,
While every leaf that His plumes touch
     Saith His Name audibly.

"And I myself will teach to him,
     I myself, lying so,
The songs I sing here; which his voice
     Shall pause in, hushed and slow,
And find some knowledge at each pause,
     Or some new thing to know."

(Alas! we two, we two, thou say'st!
     Yea, one wast though with me
That once of old. But shall God lift
     To endless unity
The soul whose likeness with thy soul
     Was but its love for thee?)

"We two," she said, "will seek the groves
     Where the lady Mary is,
With her five handmaidens, whose names
     Are five sweet symphonies,
Cecily, Gertrude, Magdalen,
     Margaret and Rosalys.

"Circlewise sit they, with bound locks
     And foreheads garlanded;
Into the fine cloth white like flame
     Weaving the golden thread,
To fashion the birth-robes for them
     Who are just born, being dead.

"He shall fear, haply, and be dumb:
   Then will I lay my cheek
To his, and tell about our love,
   Not once abashed or weak:
And the dear Mother will approve
   My pride, and let me speak.

"Herself shall bring us, hand in hand,
   To Him round whom all souls
Kneel, the clear-ranged unnumbered heads
   Bowed with their aureoles:
And angels meeting us shall sing
   To their citherns and citoles.

"There will I ask of Christ the Lord
   Thus much for him and me:
Only to live as once on earth
   With Love—only to be,
As then awhile, for ever now
   Together, I and he."

She gazed and listened and then said,
   Less sad of speech than mild—
"All this is when he comes." She ceased.
   The light thrilled towards her, fill'd
With angels in strong level flight.
   Her eyes prayed, and she smil'd.

(I saw her smile.) But soon their path
   Was vague in distant spheres:
And then she cast her arms along
   The golden barriers,
And laid her face between her hands,
   And wept. (I heard her tears.)

My Sister's Sleep

SHE fell asleep on Christmas Eve.
  At length the long-ungranted shade
  Of weary eyelids overweigh'd
The pain nought else might yet relieve.

Our mother, who had leaned all day
  Over the bed from chime to chime,
  Then raised herself for the first time,
And as she sat her down, did pray.

Her little work-table was spread
  With work to finish. For the glare
  Made by her candle, she had care
To work some distance from the bed.

Without, there was a cold moon up,
  Of winter radiance sheer and thin;
  The hollow halo it was in
Was like an icy crystal cup.

Through the small room, with subtle sound
  Of flame, by vents the fireshine drove
  And reddened. In its dim alcove
The mirror shed a clearness round.

I had been sitting up some nights,
  And my tired mind felt weak and blank;
  Like a sharp strengthening wine it drank
The stillness and the broken lights.

Twelve struck. That sound, by dwindling years
  Heard in each hour, crept off; and then
  The ruffled silence spread again,
Like water that a pebble stirs.

Our mother rose from where she sat:
   Her needles, as she laid them down,
   Met lightly, and her silken gown
Settled: no other noise than that.

"Glory unto the Newly Born!"
   So, as said angels, she did say,
   Because we were in Christmas Day,
Though it would still be long till morn.

Just then in the room over us
   There was a pushing back of chairs,
   As some who had sat unawares
So late, now heard the hour, and rose.

With anxious softly-stepping haste
   Our mother went where Margaret lay,
   Fearing the sounds o'erhead—should they
Have broken her long watched-for rest!

She stooped an instant, calm, and turned;
   But suddenly turned back again;
   And all her features seemed in pain
With woe, and her eyes gazed and yearned.

For my part, I but hid my face,
   And held my breath, and spoke no word:
   There was none spoken; but I heard
The silence for a little space.

Our mother bowed herself and wept:
   And both my arms fell, and I said,
   "God knows I knew that she was dead."
And there, all white, my sister slept.

Then kneeling, upon Christmas morn
A little after twelve o'clock,
We said, ere the first quarter struck,
"Christ's blessing on the newly born!"

SUDDEN LIGHT

I have been here before,
But when or how I cannot tell:
I know the grass beyond the door,
The sweet keen smell,
The sighing sound, the lights around the shore.

You have been mine before—
How long ago I may not know:
But just when at that swallow's soar
Your neck turned so,
Some veil did fall—I knew it all of yore.

Has this been thus before?
And shall not thus time's eddying flight
Still with our lives our love restore
In death's despite,
And day and night yield one delight once more?

SISTER HELEN

"Why did you melt your waxen man,
Sister Helen?
To-day is the third since you began."
"The time was long, yet the time ran,
Little brother."
(*O Mother, Mary Mother,*
Three days to-day, between Hell and Heaven!)

"But if you have done your work aright,
            Sister Helen,
You'll let me play, for you said I might."
"Be very still in your play to-night,
            Little brother."
            (*O Mother, Mary Mother,*
Third night, to-night, between Hell and Heaven!)

"You said it must melt ere vesper-bell,
            Sister Helen;
If now it be molten, all is well."
"Even so—nay, peace! you cannot tell,
            Little brother."
            (*O Mother, Mary Mother,*
O what is this, between Hell and Heaven?)

"Oh the waxen knave was plump to-day,
            Sister Helen;
How like dead folk he has dropped away!"
"Nay now, of the dead what can you say,
            Little brother?"
            (*O Mother, Mary Mother,*
What of the dead, between Hell and Heaven?)

"See, see, the sunken pile of wood,
            Sister Helen,
Shines through the thinned wax red as blood!"
"Nay now, when looked you yet on blood,
            Little brother?"
            (*O Mother, Mary Mother,*
How pale she is, between Hell and Heaven!)

"Now close your eyes, for they're sick and sore,
            Sister Helen,
And I'll play without the gallery door."

"Aye, let me rest—I'll lie on the floor,
Little brother."
(*O Mother, Mary Mother,*
What rest to-night, between Hell and Heaven?)

"Here high up in the balcony,
Sister Helen,
The moon flies face to face with me."
"Aye, look and say whatever you see,
Little brother."
(*O Mother, Mary Mother,*
What sight to-night, between Hell and Heaven?)

"Outside it's merry in the wind's wake,
Sister Helen;
In the shaken trees the chill stars shake."
"Hush, heard you a horse-tread as you spake,
Little brother?"
(*O Mother, Mary Mother,*
What sound to-night, between Hell and Heaven?)

"I hear a horse-tread, and I see,
Sister Helen,
Three horsemen that ride terribly."
"Little brother, whence come the three,
Little brother?"
(*O Mother, Mary Mother,*
Whence should they come, between Hell and Heaven?)

"They come by the hill-verge from Boyne Bar,
Sister Helen,
And one draws nigh, but two are afar."
"Look, look, do you know them who they are,
Little brother?"
(*O Mother, Mary Mother,*
Who should they be, between Hell and Heaven?)

"Oh, it's Keith of Eastholm rides so fast,
      Sister Helen,
For I know the white mane on the blast."
"The hour has come, has come at last,
      Little brother!"
    (O Mother, Mary Mother,
Her hour at last, between Hell and Heaven!)

"He has made a sign and called Halloo!
      Sister Helen,
And he says that he would speak with you."
"Oh tell him I fear the frozen dew,
      Little brother."
    (O Mother, Mary Mother,
Why laughs she thus, between Hell and Heaven?)

"The wind is loud, but I hear him cry,
      Sister Helen,
That Keith of Ewern's like to die."
"And he and thou, and thou and I,
      Little brother."
    (O Mother, Mary Mother,
And they and we, between Hell and Heaven!)

"Three days ago, on his marriage-morn,
      Sister Helen,
He sickened, and lies since then forlorn."
"For bridegroom's side is the bride a thorn,
      Little brother?"
    (O Mother, Mary Mother,
Cold bridal cheer, between Hell and Heaven!)

"Three days and nights he has lain abed,
      Sister Helen,
And he prays in torment to be dead."

"The thing may chance, if he have prayed,
            Little brother!"
        (*O Mother, Mary Mother,*
If he have prayed, between Hell and Heaven!)

"But he has not ceased to cry to-day,
            Sister Helen,
That you should take your curse away."
"My prayer was heard—he need but pray,
            Little brother!"
        (*O Mother, Mary Mother,*
Shall God not hear, between Hell and Heaven?)

"But he says, till you take back your ban,
            Sister Helen,
His soul would pass, yet never can."
"Nay then, shall I slay a living man,
            Little brother?"
        (*O Mother, Mary Mother,*
A living soul, between Hell and Heaven!)

"But he calls for ever on your name,
            Sister Helen,
And says that he melts before a flame."
"My heart for his pleasure fared the same,
            Little brother."
        (*O Mother, Mary Mother,*
Fire at the Heart, between Hell and Heaven!)

"Here's Keith of Westholm riding fast,
            Sister Helen,
For I know the white plume on the blast."
"The hour, the sweet hour I forecast,
            Little brother!"
        (*O Mother, Mary Mother,*
Is the hour sweet, between Hell and Heaven?)

"He stops to speak, and he stills his horse,
                Sister Helen;
But his words are drowned in the wind's course."
"Nay hear, nay hear, you must hear perforce,
                Little brother!"
            (*O Mother, Mary Mother*
What word now heard, between Hell and Heaven?)

"Oh he says that Keith of Ewern's cry,
                Sister Helen,
Is ever to see you ere he die."
"In all that his soul sees, there am I,
                Little brother!"
            (*O Mother, Mary Mother,*
The soul's one sight, between Hell and Heaven!)

"He sends a ring and a broken coin,
                Sister Helen,
And bids you mind the banks of Boyne."
"What else he broke will he ever join,
                Little brother?"
            (*O Mother, Mary Mother,*
No, never joined, between Hell and Heaven!)

"He yields you these and craves full fain,
                Sister Helen,
You pardon him in his mortal pain."
"What else he took will he give again,
                Little brother?"
            (*O Mother, Mary Mother,*
Not twice to give, between Hell and Heaven!)

"He calls your name in an agony,
                Sister Helen,
That even dead Love must weep to see."

"Hate, born of Love, is blind as he,
            Little brother!"
        (*O Mother, Mary Mother,*
Love turned to hate, between Hell and Heaven!)

"Oh it's Keith of Keith now that rides fast,
            Sister Helen,
For I know the white hair on the blast."
"The short short hour will soon be past,
            Little brother!"
        (*O Mother, Mary Mother,*
Will soon be past, between Hell and Heaven!)

"He looks at me and he tries to speak,
            Sister Helen,
But oh! his voice is sad and weak!"
"What here should the mighty Baron seek,
            Little brother?"
        (*O Mother, Mary Mother,*
Is this the end, between Hell and Heaven?)

"Oh his son still cries, if you forgive,
            Sister Helen,
The body dies but the soul shall live."
"Fire shall forgive me as I forgive,
            Little brother!"
        (*O Mother, Mary Mother,*
As she forgives, between Hell and Heaven!)

"Oh he prays you, as his heart would rive,
            Sister Helen,
To save his dear son's soul alive."
"Fire cannot slay it, it shall thrive,
            Little brother!"
        (*O Mother, Mary Mother,*
Alas, alas, between Hell and Heaven!)

"He cries to you, kneeling in the road,
        Sister Helen,
To go with him for the love of God!"
"The way is long to his son's abode,
        Little brother."
        (O Mother, Mary Mother,
The way is long, between Hell and Heaven!)

"A lady's here, by a dark steed brought,
        Sister Helen,
So darkly clad, I saw her not."
"See her now or never see aught,
        Little brother!"
        (O Mother, Mary Mother,
What more to see, between Hell and Heaven?)

"Her hood falls back, and the moon shines fair,
        Sister Helen,
On the Lady of Ewern's golden hair."
"Blest hour of my power and her despair,
        Little brother!"
        (O Mother, Mary Mother,
Hour blest and bann'd, between Hell and Heaven!)

"Pale, pale her cheeks, that in pride did glow,
        Sister Helen,
'Neath the bridal wreath three days ago."
"One morn for pride and three days for woe,
        Little brother!"
        (O Mother, Mary Mother,
Three days, three nights, between Hell and Heaven!)

"Her clasped hands stretch from her bending head,
        Sister Helen;
With the loud wind's wail her sobs are wed."

"What wedding-strains hath her bridal-bed,
                    Little brother?"
            (*O Mother, Mary Mother,*
What strain but death's, between Hell and Heaven?)

"She may not speak, she sinks in a swoon,
                    Sister Helen—
She lifts her lips and gasps on the moon."
"Oh! might I but hear her soul's blithe tune,
                    Little brother!"
            (*O Mother, Mary Mother,*
Her woe's dumb cry, between Hell and Heaven!)

"'They've caught her to Westholm's saddle-bow,
                    Sister Helen,
And her moonlit hair gleams white in its flow."
"Let it turn whiter than winter snow,
                    Little brother!"
            (*O Mother, Mary Mother,*
Woe-withered gold, between Hell and Heaven!)

"O Sister Helen, you heard the bell,
                    Sister Helen!
More loud than the vesper-chime it fell."
"No vesper-chime, but a dying knell,
                    Little brother!"
            (*O Mother, Mary Mother,*
His dying knell, between Hell and Heaven!)

"Alas, but I fear the heavy sound,
                    Sister Helen;
Is it in the sky or in the ground?"
"Say, have they turned their horses round,
                    Little brother?"
            (*O Mother, Mary Mother,*
What would she more, between Hell and Heaven?)

THE AWAKENED CONSCIENCE
W. Holman Hunt

WORK
Ford Madox Brown

"They have raised the old man from his knee,
            Sister Helen,
And they ride in silence hastily."
"More fast the naked soul doth flee,
            Little brother!"
            (*O Mother, Mary Mother,*
The naked soul, between Hell and Heaven!)

"Flank to flank are the three steeds gone,
            Sister Helen,
But the lady's dark steed goes alone."
"And lonely her bridegroom's soul hath flown,
            Little brother."
            (*O Mother, Mary Mother,*
The lonely ghost, between Hell and Heaven!)

"Oh the wind is sad in the iron chill,
            Sister Helen,
And weary sad they look by the hill."
"But he and I are sadder still,
            Little brother!"
            (*O Mother, Mary Mother,*
Most sad of all, between Hell and Heaven!)

"See, see, the wax has dropped from its place,
            Sister Helen,
And the flames are winning up apace!"
"Yet here they burn but for a space,
            Little brother!"
            (*O Mother, Mary Mother,*
Here for a space between Hell and Heaven!)

"Ah! What white thing at the door has cross'd,
            Sister Helen?
Ah! What is this that sighs in the frost?"

"A soul that's lost as mine is lost,
        Little brother!"
        (*O Mother, Mary Mother,
Lost, lost, all lost, between Hell and Heaven!*)

FROM "A LAST CONFESSION"

SHE had a mouth
Made to bring death to life—the underlip
Sucked in, as if it strove to kiss itself.
Her face was pearly pale, as when one stoops
Over wan water; and the dark crisped hair
And the hair's shadow made it paler still—
Deep-serried locks, the dimness of the cloud
Where the moon's gaze is set in eddying gloom.
Her body bore her neck as the tree's stem
Bears the top branch; and as the branch sustains
The flower of the year's pride, her high neck bore
That face made wonderful with night and day.
Her voice was swift, yet ever the last words
Fell lingeringly; and rounded finger-tips
She had, that clung a little where they touched
And then were gone o' the instant. Her great eyes
That sometimes turned half-dizzily beneath
The passionate lids, as faint, when she would speak,
Had also in them hidden springs of mirth,
Which under the dark lashes evermore
Shook to her laugh, as when a bird flies low
Between the water and the willow-leaves,
And the shade quivers till he wins the light.

From "The House of Life"

LOVESIGHT

WHEN do I see thee most, beloved one?
  When in the light the spirits of mine eyes
  Before thy face, their altar, solemnize
The worship of that Love through thee made known?
Or when in the dusk hours, (we two alone,)
  Close-kissed and eloquent of still replies
  Thy twilight-hidden glimmering visage lies,
And my soul only sees thy soul its own?

O love, my love! if I no more should see
Thyself, nor on the earth the shadow of thee,
  Nor image of thine eyes in any spring—
How then should sound upon Life's darkening slope
The ground-whirl of the perished leaves of Hope,
  The wind of Death's imperishable wing?

THE PORTRAIT

O LORD of all compassionate control,
  O Love! Let this my lady's picture glow
  Under my hand to praise her name, and show
Even of her inner self the perfect whole:
That he who seeks her beauty's furthest goal,
  Beyond the light that the sweet glances throw
  And refluent wave of the sweet smile, may know
The very sky and sea-line of her soul.

Lo! it is done. Above the enthroning throat
  The mouth's mould testifies of voice and kiss,
    The shadowed eyes remember and foresee.

Her face is made her shrine. Let all men note
That in all years (O Love, thy gift is this!)
They that would look on her must come to me.

SILENT NOON

Your hands lie open in the long fresh grass—
The finger-points look through like rosy blooms:
Your eyes smile peace. The pasture gleams and glooms
'Neath billowing skies that scatter and amass.
All round our nest, far as the eye can pass,
Are golden kingcup-fields with silver edge
Where the cow-parsley skirts the hawthorn-hedge.
'Tis visible silence, still as the hour-glass.

Deep in the sun-searched growth the dragon-fly
Hangs like a blue thread loosened from the sky:
So this wing'd hour is dropt to us from above.
Oh! clasp we to our hearts, for deathless dower,
This close-companioned inarticulate hour
When twofold silence was the song of love.

HER GIFTS

HIGH grace, the dower of queens; and therewithal
Some wood-born wonder's sweet simplicity
A glance like water brimming with the sky
Or hyacinth-light where forest-shadows fall;
Such thrilling pallor of cheek as doth enthral
The heart; a mouth whose passionate forms imply
All music and all silence held thereby;
Deep golden locks, her sovereign coronal;
A round reared neck, meet column of Love's shrine

To cling to when the heart takes sanctuary;
 Hands which for ever at Love's bidding be,
And soft-stirred feet still answering to his sign:
These are her gifts, as tongue may tell them o'er.
Breathe low her name, my soul; for that means more.

Autumn Idleness

This sunlight shames November where he grieves
 In dead red leaves, and will not let him shun
 The day, though bough with bough be over-run.
But with a blessing every glade receives
High salutation; while from hillock-eaves
 The deer gaze calling, dappled white and dun,
 As if, being foresters of old, the sun
Had marked them with the shade of forest-leaves.

Here dawn to-day unveiled her magic glass;
 Here noon now gives the thirst and takes the dew;
Till eve bring rest when other good things pass.
 And here the lost hours the lost hours renew
While I still lead my shadow o'er the grass,
 Nor know, for longing, that which I should do.

Jenny

"Vengeance of Jenny's case! Fie on her!
Never name her, child!"—*Mrs Quickly*.

Lazy laughing languid Jenny,
 Fond of a kiss and fond of a guinea,
 Whose head upon my knee tonight
 Rests for a while, as if grown light

With all our dances and the sound
To which the wild tunes spun you round:
Fair Jenny mine, the thoughtless queen
Of kisses which the blush between
Could hardly make much daintier;

Whose eyes are as blue skies, whose hair
Is countless gold incomparable:
Fresh flower, scarce touched with signs that tell
Of Love's exuberant hotbed—nay,
Poor flower left torn since yesterday
Until to-morrow leave you bare;
Poor handful of bright spring-water
Flung in the whirlpool's shrieking face;
Poor shameful Jenny, full of grace
Thus with your head upon my knee—
Whose person or whose purse may be
The lodestar of your reverie?

This room of yours, my Jenny, looks
A change from mine, so full of books
Whose serried ranks hold fast, forsooth,
So many captive hours of youth—
The hours they thieve from day and night
To make one's cherished work come right,
And leave it wrong for all their theft,
Even as to-night my work was left:
Until I vowed that since my brain
And eyes of dancing seemed so fain,
My feet should have some dancing too—
And thus it was I met with you.
Well, I suppose 'twas hard to part,
For here I am. And now, sweetheart,
You seem too tired to get to bed.

It was a careless life I led
When rooms like this were scarce so strange
Not long ago. What breeds the change—
The many aims or the few years?
Because to-night it all appears
Something I do not know again.

The cloud's not danced out of my brain—
The cloud that made it turn and swim
While hour by hour the books grew dim.
Why, Jenny, as I watch you there—
For all your wealth of loosened hair,
Your silk ungirdled and unlac'd
And warm sweets open to the waist,
All golden in the lamplight's gleam—
You know not what a book you seem,
Half-read by lightning in a dream!
How should you know, my Jenny? Nay,
And I should be ashamed to say—
Poor beauty, so well worth a kiss!
But while my thought runs on like this
With wasteful whims more than enough,
I wonder what you're thinking of.

If of myself you think at all,
What is the thought?—conjectural
On sorry matters best unsolved?—
Or inly is each grace revolved
To fit me with a lure?—or (sad
To think!) perhaps you're merely glad
That I'm not drunk or ruffianly
And let you rest upon my knee.

For sometimes, were the truth confess'd,
You're thankful for a little rest—

Glad from the crush to rest within,
From the heart-sickness and the din
Where envy's voice at virtue's pitch
Mocks you because your gown is rich;
And from the pale girl's dumb rebuke,
Whose ill-clad grace and toil-worn look,
Proclaim the strength that keeps her weak,
And other nights than yours bespeak;
And from the wise unchildish elf,
To schoolmate lesser than himself
Pointing you out, what thing you are—
Yes, from the daily jeer and jar,
For shame and shame's outbraving too,
Is rest not sometimes sweet to you?—
But most from the hatefulness of man,
Who spares not to end what he began,
Whose acts are ill and his speech ill,
Who, having used you at his will,
Thrusts you aside, as when I dine
I serve the dishes and the wine.

Well, handsome Jenny mine, sit up:
I've filled our glasses, let me sup,
And do not let me think of you,
Lest shame of yours suffice for two.
What, still so tired? Well, well then, keep
Your head there, so you do not sleep;
But that the weariness may pass
And leave you merry, take this glass.
Ah! lazy lily hand, more bless'd
If ne'er in rings it had been dress'd
Nor ever by a glove conceal'd!

Behold the lilies of the field,
They toil not neither do they spin;

(So doth the ancient text begin—
Not of such rest as one of these
Can share.) Another rest and ease
Along each summer-sated path
From its new lord the garden hath,
Than that whose spring in blessings ran
Which praised the bounteous husbandman,
Ere yet, in days of hankering breath,
The lilies sickened unto death.

What, Jenny, are your lilies dead?
Aye, and the snow-white leaves are spread
Like winter on the garden-bed.
But you had roses left in May—
They were not gone too. Jenny, nay,
But must your roses die, and those
Their purfled buds that should unclose?
Even so; the leaves are curled apart,
Still red as from the broken heart,
And here's the naked stem of thorns.

Nay, nay, mere words. Here nothing warns
As yet of winter. Sickness here
Or want alone could waken fear—
Nothing but passion wrings a tear.
Except when there may rise unsought
Haply at times a passing thought
Of the old days which seem to be
Much older than any history
That is written in any book;
When she would lie in fields and look
Along the ground through the blown grass,
And wonder where the city was,
Far out of sight, whose broil and bale
They told her then for a child's tale.

Jenny, you know the city now.
A child can tell the tale there, how
Some things which are not yet enroll'd
In market-lists are bought and sold
Even till the early Sunday light,
When Saturday night is market-night
Everywhere, be it dry or wet,
And market-night in the Haymarket.
Our learned London children know,
Poor Jenny, all your pride and woe;
Have seen your lifted silken skirt
Advertise dainties through the dirt;
Have seen your coach-wheels splash rebuke
On virtue; and have learned your look
When, wealth and health slipped past, you stare
Along the streets alone, and there,
Round the long park, across the bridge,
The cold lamps at the pavement's edge
Wind on together and apart,
A fiery serpent for your heart.

Let the thoughts pass, an empty cloud!
Suppose I were to think aloud—
What if to her all this were said?
Why, as a volume seldom read
Being opened halfway shuts again,
So might the pages of her brain
Be parted at such words, and thence
Close back upon the dusty sense.
For is there hue or shape defin'd
In Jenny's desecrated mind,
Where all contagious currents meet,
A Lethe of the middle street?
Nay, it reflects not any face,
Nor sound is in its sluggish pace,

But as they coil those eddies clot
And night and day remember not.

Why, Jenny, you're asleep at last!—
Asleep, poor Jenny, hard and fast—
So young and soft and tired; so fair,
With chin thus nestled in your hair,
Mouth quiet, eyelids almost blue
As if some sky of dreams shone through!

Just as another woman sleeps!
Enough to throw one's thoughts in heaps
Of doubt and horror—what to say
Or think—this awful secret sway,
The potter's power over the clay!
Of the same lump (it has been said)
For honour and dishonour made
Two sister vessels. Here is one.

My cousin Nell is fond of fun,
And fond of dress, and change, and praise,
So mere a woman in her ways:
And if her sweet eyes rich in youth
Are like her lips that tell the truth,
My cousin Nell is fond of love.
And she's the girl I'm proudest of.
Who does not prize her, guard her well?
The love of change, in cousin Nell,
Shall find the best and hold it dear:
The unconquered mirth turn quieter
Not through her own, through others' woe:
The conscious pride of beauty glow
Beside another's pride in her,
One little part of all they share.
For Love himself shall ripen these

In a kind soil to just increase
Through years of fertilizing peace.

Of the same lump (as it is said)
For honour and dishonour made,
Two sister vessels. Here is one.

It makes a goblin of the sun.

So pure—so fall'n! How dare to think
Of the first common kindred link?
Yet, Jenny, till the world shall burn
It seems that all things take their turn;
And who shall say but this fair tree
May need, in changes that may be,
Your children's children's charity?
Scorned then, no doubt, as you are scorned!
Shall no man hold his pride forewarn'd
Till in the end, the Day of Days,
At Judgment, one of his own race,
As frail and lost as you, shall rise—
His daughter, with his mother's eyes?

How Jenny's clock ticks on the shelf!
Might not the dial scorn itself
That has such hours to register?
Yet as to me, even so to her
Are golden sun and silver moon,
In daily largesse of earth's boon.
Counted for life-coins to one tune.
And if, as blindfold fates are toss'd,
Through some one man this life be lost,
Shall soul not somehow pay for soul?

Fair shines the gilded aureole
In which our highest painters place

Some living woman's simple face.
And the stilled features thus descried
As Jenny's long throat droops aside—
The shadows where the cheeks are thin,
And pure wide curve from ear to chin—
With Raffael's, Leonardo's hand
To show them to men's souls, might stand,
Whole ages long, the whole world through,
For preaching of what God can do.
What has man done here? How atone,
Great God, for this which man has done?
And for the body and soul which by
Man's pitiless doom must now comply
With lifelong hell, what lullaby
O sweet forgetful second birth
Remains? All dark. No sign on earth
What measure of God's rest endows
The many mansions of his house.

If but a woman's heart might see
Such erring heart unerringly
For once! But that can never be.

Like a rose shut in a book
In which pure women may not look,
For its base pages claim control
To crush the flower within the soul;
Where through each dead rose-leaf that clings,
Pale as transparent Psyche-wings,
To the vile text, are traced such things
As might make lady's cheek indeed
More than a living rose to read;
So nought save foolish foulness may
Watch with hard eyes the sure decay;
And so the life-blood of this rose,

Puddled with shameful knowledge, flows
Through leaves no chaste hand may unclose:
Yet still it keeps such faded show
Of when 'twas gathered long ago,
That the crushed petals' lovely grain,
The sweetness of the sanguine stain,
Seen of a woman's eyes, must make
Her pitiful heart, so prone to ache,
Love roses better for its sake—
Only that this can never be—
Even so unto her sex is she.

Yet, Jenny, looking long at you,
The woman almost fades from view.
A cipher of man's changeless sum
Of lust, past, present, and to come,
Is left. A riddle that one shrinks
To challenge from the scornful sphinx.

Like a toad within a stone
Seated while Time crumbles on;
Which sits there since the earth was curs'd
For Man's transgression at the first;
Which, living through all centuries,
Not once has seen the sun arise;
Whose life, to its cold circle charmed,
The earth's whole summers have not warmed;
Which always—whitherso the stone
Be flung—sits there, deaf, blind, alone;
Aye, and shall not be driven out
Till that which shuts him round about
Break at the very Master's stroke,
And the dust thereof vanish as smoke,
And the seed of Man vanish as dust—
Even so within this world is Lust.

Come, come, what use in thoughts like this?
Poor little Jenny, good to kiss—
You'd not believe by what strange roads
Thought travels, when your beauty goads
A man to-night to think of toads!
Jenny, wake up. . . . Why, there's the dawn!

And there's an early waggon drawn
To market, and some sheep that jog
Bleating before a barking dog;
And the old streets come peering through
Another night that London knew,
And all as ghostlike as the lamps.

So on the wings of day decamps
My last night's frolic. Glooms begin
To shiver off as lights creep in
Past the gauze curtains half drawn-to,
And the lamp's doubled shade grows blue—
Your lamp, my Jenny, kept alight,
Like a wise virgin's, all one night!
And in the alcove coolly spread
Glimmers with dawn your empty bed;
And yonder your fair face I see
Reflected lying on my knee,
Where teems with first foreshadowings
Your pier glass scrawled with diamond rings:
And on your bosom all night worn
Yesterday's rose now droops forlorn,
But dies not yet this summer morn.

And now without, as if some word
Had called upon them that they heard,
The London sparrows far and nigh
Clamour together suddenly;

And Jenny's cage-bird grown awake
Here in their song his part must take,
Because here too the day doth break.

And somehow in myself the dawn
Among stirred clouds and veils withdrawn
Strikes greyly on her. Let her sleep.
But will it wake her if I heap
These cushions thus beneath her head
Where my knee was? No, there's your bed,
My Jenny, while you dream. And there
I lay among your golden hair
Perhaps the subject of your dreams,
These golden coins.
                        For still one deems
That Jenny's flattering sleep confers
New magic on the magic purse—
Grim web, how clogged with shrivelled flies
Between the threads fine fumes arise
And shape their pictures in the brain.
There roll no streets in glare and rain,
Nor flagrant man-swine whets his tusk;
But delicately sighs in musk
The homage of the dim boudoir;
Or like a palpitating star
Thrilled into song, the opera-night
Breathes faint in the quick pulse of light;
Or at the carriage-window shine
Rich wares for choice; or, free to dine,
Whirls through its hour of health (divine
For her) the concourse of the Park.
And though in the discounted dark
Her functions there and here are one,
Beneath the lamps and in the sun
There reigns at least the acknowledged belle

THE GIRLHOOD OF MARY VIRGIN
D. G. Rossetti

THE MAIDS OF ELFIN-MERE
D. G. Rossetti

FOUND
D. G. Rossetti

Apparelled beyond parallel.
Ah Jenny, yes, we know your dreams.

For even the Paphian Venus seems
A goddess o'er the realms of love,
When silver-shrined in shadowy grove:
Aye, or let offerings nicely plac'd
But hide Priapus to the waist,
And whoso looks on him shall see
An eligible deity.

Why, Jenny, waking here alone
May help you to remember one,
Though all the memory's long outworn
Of many a double-pillowed morn.
I think I see you when you wake,
And rub your eyes for me, and shake
My gold, in rising, from your hair,
A Danaë for a moment there.

Jenny, my love rang true! for still
Love at first sight is vague, until
That tinkling makes him audible.

And must I mock you to the last,
Ashamed of my own shame—aghast
Because some thoughts not born amiss
Rose at a poor fair face like this?
Well, of such thoughts, so much I know:
In my life, as in hers, they show,
By a far gleam which I may near,
A dark path I can strive to clear.

Only one kiss. Good-bye, my dear.

Sonnets for Pictures

FOUND

"THERE is a budding morrow in midnight"—
   So sang our Keats, our English nightingale.
   And here, as lamps across the bridge turn pale
In London's smokeless resurrection-light,
Dark breaks to dawn. But o'er the deadly blight
   Of Love deflowered and sorrow of none avail,
   Which makes this man gasp and this woman quail,
Can day from darkness ever again take flight?

Ah! gave not these two hearts their mutual pledge,
Under one mantle sheltered 'neath the hedge
   In gloaming courtship? And, O God! to-day
He only knows he holds her; but what part
   Can life now take? She cries in her locked heart,
   "Leave me—I do not know you—go away!"

MARY'S GIRLHOOD

I

THIS is that blessed Mary, pre-elect
   God's Virgin. Gone is a great while, and she
   Dwelt young in Nazareth of Galilee.
Unto God's will she brought devout respect,
Profound simplicity of intellect,
   And supreme patience. From her mother's knee
   Faithful and hopeful; wise in charity;
Strong in grave peace; in pity circumspect.

So held she through her girlhood; as it were
   An angel-watered lily, that near God

Grows and is quiet. Till, one dawn at home
She woke in her white bed, and had no fear
At all—yet wept till sunshine, and felt awed:
Because the fulness of the time was come.

II

These are the symbols. On that cloth of red
I' the centre is the Tripoint: perfect each,
Except the second of its points, to teach
That Christ is not yet born. The books—whose head
Is golden Charity, as Paul hath said—
Those virtues are wherein the soul is rich:
Therefore on them the lily standeth, which
Is innocence, being interpreted.

The seven-thorn'd briar and the palm seven-leaved
Are her great sorrow and her great reward.
Until the end be full, the Holy One
Abides without. She soon shall have achieved
Her perfect purity: yea, God the Lord
Shall soon vouchsafe His Son to be her Son.

CHRISTINA ROSSETTI

FROM "GOBLIN MARKET"

GOLDEN head by golden head,
Like two pigeons in one nest
Folded in each other's wings,
They lay down in their curtained bed;
Like two blossoms on one stem,
Like two flakes of new-fall'n snow,
Like two wands of ivory
Tipped with gold for awful kings.

GOBLIN MARKET

D. G. Rossetti

Moon and stars gazed in at them,
Wind sang to them lullaby,
Lumbering owls forebore to fly,
Not a bat flapped to and fro
Round their rest:
Cheek to cheek and breast to breast
Locked together in one nest.

Early in the morning
When the first cock crowed his warning,
Neat like bees, as sweet and busy,
Laura rose with Lizzie:
Fetched in honey, milked the cows,
Aired and set to rights the house,

Kneaded cakes of whitest wheat,
Cakes for dainty mouths to eat,
Next churned butter, whipped up cream,
Fed their poultry, sat and sewed;
Talked as modest maidens should:
Lizzie with an open heart,
Laura in an absent dream,
One content, one sick in part;
One warbling for the mere bright day's delight,
One longing for the night.

A BIRTHDAY

My heart is like a singing bird
   Whose nest is in a watered shoot;
My heart is like an apple-tree
   Whose boughs are bent with thickset fruit;
My heart is like a rainbow shell
   That paddles in a halcyon sea;
My heart is gladder than all these
   Because my love is come to me.

Raise me a dais of silk and down;
   Hang it with vair and purple dyes;
Carve it in doves and pomegranates,
   And peacocks with a hundred eyes;
Work it in gold and silver grapes,
   In leaves and silver fleur-de-lys;
Because the birthday of my life
   Is come, my love is come to me.

ECHO

COME to me in the silence of the night;
   Come in the speaking silence of a dream;
Come with soft rounded cheeks and eyes as bright
    As sunlight on a stream;
      Come back in tears,
O memory, hope, love of finished years.

O dream how sweet, too sweet, too bitter sweet,
   Whose wakening should have been in Paradise,
Where souls brimfull of love abide and meet;
    Where thirsting longing eyes
      Watch the slow door
That opening, letting in, lets out no more.

Yet come to me in dreams, that I may live
   My very life again though cold in death:
Come back to me in dreams, that I may give
    Pulse for pulse, breath for breath:
      Speak low, lean low,
As long ago, my love, how long ago.

REMEMBER

REMEMBER me when I am gone away,
   Gone far away into the silent land;
   When you can no more hold me by the hand,
Nor I half turn to go yet turning stay.
Remember me when no more day by day
   You tell me of our future that you planned:
   Only remember me; you understand
It will be late to counsel then or pray.
Yet if you should forget me for a while

And afterwards remember, do not grieve:
For if the darkness and corruption leave
A vestige of the thoughts that once I had,
Better by far you should forget and smile
Than that you should remember and be sad.

SING-SONG

Arthur Hughes

FROM "SING-SONG"

IF the moon came from heaven,
   Talking all the way,
What could she have to tell us,
   And what could she say?

"I've seen a hundred pretty things,
 And seen a hundred gay;
But only think: I peep by night
 And do not peep by day!"

WILLIAM ALLINGHAM

THE MAIDS OF ELFIN-MERE

'TWAS when the spinning-room was here.
Came Three Damsels clothed in white,
With their spindles every night;
Two and one, and Three fair Maidens,
Spinning to a pulsing cadence,
Singing songs of Elfin-Mere;
Till the eleventh hour was toll'd,
Then departed through the wold.
 Years ago, and years ago;
 And the tall reeds sigh as the wind doth blow.

Three white Lilies, calm and clear,
And they were loved by every one;
Most of all, the Pastor's Son,
Listening to their gentle singing,
Felt his heart go from him, clinging
Round these Maids of Elfin-Mere;
Sued each night to make them stay,
Sadden'd when they went away.
 Years ago, and years ago;
 And the tall reeds sigh as the wind doth blow.

Hands that shook with love and fear
Dared put back the village clock—
Flew the spindle, turn'd the rock,

Flow'd the song with subtle rounding,
Till the false "eleven" was sounding;
Then these Maids of Elfin-Mere
Swiftly, softly, left the room,
Like three doves on snowy plume.
  Years ago, and years ago;
  And the tall reeds sigh as the wind doth blow.

One that night who wander'd near
Heard lamenting by the shore,
Saw at dawn three stains of gore
In the waters fade and dwindle.
Nevermore with song and spindle
Saw we Maids of Elfin-Mere.
The Pastor's Son did pine and die;
Because true love should never lie.
  Years ago, and years ago;
  And the tall reeds sigh as the wind doth blow.

IN A SPRING GROVE

HERE the white-ray'd anemone is born,
Wood-sorrel, and the varnish'd buttercup;
And primrose in its purfled green swathed up,
Pallid and sweet round every budding thorn,
Gray ash, and beech with rusty leaves outworn.
Here, too, the darting linnet has her nest
In the blue-lustred holly, never shorn,
Whose partner cheers her little brooding breast,
Piping from some near bough. O simple song!
O cistern deep of that harmonious rillet,
And these fair juicy stems that climb and throng
The vernal world, and unexhausted seas
Of flowing life, and soul that asks to fill it,
Each and all these—and more, and more, than these!

O UNKNOWN BELOV'D ONE

O Unknown Belov'd One! to the mellow season
    Branches in the lawn make drooping bow'rs;
  Vase and plot burn scarlet, gold and azure;
  Honeysuckles wind the tall gray turret,
    And pale passion-flow'rs.
  Come thou, come thou to my lonely thought,
     O Unknown Belov'd One.

Now, at evening twilight, dusky dew down-wavers,
    Soft stars crown the grove-encircled hill;
  Breathe the new-mown meadows, broad and misty;
  Through the heavy grass the rail is talking;
    All beside is still.
  Trace with me the wandering avenue,
     Thou Unknown Belov'd One.

In the mystic realm, and in the time of visions,
    I thy lover have no need to woo;
  There I hold thy hand in mine, thou dearest,
  And thy soul in mine, and feel it throbbing,
    Tender, deep and true:
  Then my tears are love, and thine are love,
     Thou Unknown Belov'd One.

Is thy voice a wavelet on the listening darkness?
    Are thine eyes unfolding from their veil?
  Wilt thou come before the signs of winter—
  Days that shred the boughs with trembling fingers,
    Nights that weep and wail?
  Art thou Love indeed, or art thou Death,
     O Unknown Belov'd One?

WILLIAM BELL SCOTT

From "Green Cherries"

I swung
The gate and entered. All along the edge
Of the bright gravel fallen lilac blooms
Or young leaf-sheaths were scattered, and small groups
Of coming toadstools showed where showers had lain.
Under the wavering shades of trees I turned,
Skirting the garden's boxwood bordered ways,
Its rhododendrons bursting into flower,
Flaming beneath the sunshine, and at length
Rested upon an orchard arbour seat.

STUDIES FROM NATURE

W. Bell Scott

All over bench and table, ground and sward,
The young green cherries lay, yet overhead,
Glittering like beads, they still seemed thick as leaves
Upon the boughs. And young green apples too,
Scattered by prodigal winds, peeped here and there,
Among the clover. Through the black boughs shone
Clouds of a white heat, in the cold blue depths
Poised steadily, and all about them rang
Those songs of skylarks. Other sounds were there:
The click mistimed of hedge-shears; the brave bee
Passing with trumpet gladness; and the leaves
Waving against each other. Soon this way
Along the further hedge-top came the shears;
Two wielding arms assiduous and a face
The prickly screen disclosed. Far down the line
By slow degrees went shears and arms, while I
Marked the still toppling twigs, until at length
They passed beyond the fruit-trees, and I turned
To other themes.

FROM "THE WITCH'S BALLAD"

O, I hae come from far away,
    From a warm land far away,
A southern land across the sea,
With sailor-lads about the mast,
Merry and canny, and kind to me.

And I hae been to yon town,
    To try my luck in yon town;
Nort, and Mysie, Elspie too.
Right braw we were to pass the gate,
Wi' gowden clasps on girdles blue.

Mysie smiled wi' miminy mouth,
　Innocent mouth, miminy mouth;
Elspie wore her scarlet gown,
Nort's grey eyes were unco' gleg,
My Castile comb was like a crown.

We walked abreast all up the street,
　Into the market up the street;
Our hair with marygolds was wound,
Our bodices with love-knots laced,
Our merchandise with tansy bound.

　.　　.　　.　　.　　.　　.

[*The next fourteen stanzas describe how they bewitch the townspeople into dancing, and each of the four enchants a man for herself.*]

Drawn up I was right off my feet,
　Into the mist and off my feet;
And, dancing on each chimney-top,
I saw a thousand darling imps
Keeping time with skip and hop.

And on the provost's brave ridge-tile,
　On the provost's grand ridge-tile,
The Blackamoor first to master me
I saw—I saw that winsome smile,
The mouth that did my heart beguile,
And spoke the great Word over me,
In the land beyond the sea.

I called his name, I called aloud,
　Alas! I called on him aloud;
And then he filled his hand with stour,
And threw it towards me in the air;
My mouse flew out, I lost my pow'r!

My lusty strength, my power, were gone;
 Power was gone, and all was gone.
He will not let me love him more!
Of bell and whip and horse's tail
He cares not if I find a store.

But I am proud if he is fierce!
 I am as proud as he is fierce;
I'll turn about and backward go,
If I meet again that Blackamoor,
And he'll help us then, for he shall know
I seek another paramour.

And we'll gang once more to yon town,
 Wi' better luck to yon town;
We'll walk in silk and cramoisie,
And I shall wed the provost's son;
My-lady of the town I'll be!

For I was born a crowned king's child,
 Born and nursed a king's child,
King o' a land ayont the sea,
Where the Blackamoor kissed me first,
And taught me art and glamourie.

Each one in her wame shall hide
 Her hairy mouse, her wary mouse,
Fed on madwort and agramie—
Wear amber beads between her breasts,
And blind-worm's skin about her knee.

The Lombard shall be Elspie's man,
 Elspie's gowden husband-man;
Nort shall take the lawyer's hand;
The priest shall swear another vow;
We'll dance again the saraband!

THOMAS WOOLNER

From "My Beautiful Lady"

This is why I thought weeds were beautiful:
Because one day I saw my lady pull
    Some weeds up near a little brook,
    Which home most carefully she took,
    Then shut them in a book.

A deer when startled by the stealthy ounce,
A bird escaping from the falcon's trounce,
    Feels his heart swell as mine, when she
    Stands statelier, expecting me,
    Than tall white lilies be.

The first white flutter of her robe to trace,
Where binds and perfumed jasmine interlace,
    Expands my gaze triumphantly:
    Even such his gaze, who sees on high
    His flag, for victory.

We wander forth unconsciously, because
The azure beauty of the evening draws:
    When sober hues pervade the ground,
    And life in one vast hush seems drowned,
    Air stirs so little sound.

We thread a copse where frequent bramble spray
With loose obtrusion from the side roots stray,
    (Forcing sweet pauses on our walk);
    I'll lift one with my foot, and talk
    About its leaves and stalk.

Or may be that the prickles of some stem
Will hold a prisoner her long garment's hem;
   To disentangle it I kneel,
   Oft wounding more than I can heal;
   It makes her laugh, my zeal.

MY BEAUTIFUL LADY

W. Holman Hunt

WILLIAM MORRIS

CHAUCER

(From " The Life and Death of Jason")

So ends the winning of the Golden Fleece,
So ends the tale of that sweet rest and peace
That unto Jason and his love befell;
Another story now my tongue must tell,
And tremble in the telling. Would that I
Had but some portion of that mastery
That from the rose-hung lanes of woody Kent
Through these five hundred years such songs have sent
To us, who, meshed within this smoky net
Of unrejoicing labour, love them yet.
And thou, O Master!—Yea, my Master still,
Whatever feet have scaled Parnassus' hill,
Since like thy measures, clear, and sweet, and strong,
Thames' stream scarce fettered bore the bream along
Unto the bastioned bridge, his only chain.
O Master, pardon me, if yet in vain
'Thou art my Master, and I fail to bring
Before men's eyes the image of the thing
My heart is filled with: thou whose dreamy eyes
Beheld the flush to Cressid's cheeks arise,
When Troilus rode up the praising street,
As clearly as they saw thy townsmen meet
Those who in vineyards of Poictou withstood
The glittering horror of the steel-topped wood.

An Apology

(*From "The Earthly Paradise"*)

Of Heaven or Hell I have no power to sing,
I cannot ease the burden of your fears,
Or make quick-coming death a little thing,
Or bring again the pleasure of past years,
Nor for my words shall ye forget your tears,
Or hope again for aught that I can say,
The idle singer of an empty day.

But rather, when aweary of your mirth,
From full hearts still unsatisfied ye sigh,
And, feeling kindly unto all the earth,
Grudge every minute as it passes by,
Made the more mindful that the sweet days die—
Remember me a little then I pray,
The idle singer of an empty day.

The heavy trouble, the bewildering care
That weighs us down who live and earn our bread,
These idle verses have no power to bear;
So let me sing of names remembered,
Because they, living not, can ne'er be dead,
Or long time take their memory quite away
From us poor singers of an empty day.

Dreamer of dreams, born out of my due time,
Why should I strive to set the crooked straight?
Let it suffice me that my murmuring rhyme
Beats with light wing against the ivory gate,
Telling a tale not too importunate
To those who in the sleepy region stay,
Lulled by the singer of an empty day.

Folk say, a wizard to a northern king
At Christmas-tide such wondrous things did show,
That through one window men beheld the spring,
And through another saw the summer glow,
And through a third the fruited vines a-row,
While still, unheard, but in its wonted way,
Piped the drear wind of that December day.

So with this Earthly Paradise it is,
If ye will read aright, and pardon me,
Who strive to build a shadowy isle of bliss
Midmost the beating of the steely sea,
Where tossed about all hearts of men must be;
Whose ravening monsters mighty men shall slay,
Not the poor singer of an empty day.

Cupid finds Psyche

*(From " The Story of Cupid and Psyche" in
" The Earthly Paradise")*

Withal at last amidst a fair green close,
Hedged round about with woodbine and red rose,
Within the flicker of a white-thorn shade
In gentle sleep he found the maiden laid;
One hand that held a book had fallen away
Across her body, and the other lay
Upon a marble fountain's plashing rim,
Among whose broken waves the fish showed dim,
But yet its wide-flung spray now woke her not,
Because the summer day at noon was hot,
And all sweet sounds and scents were lulling her.
So soon the rustle of his wings 'gan stir
Her looser folds of raiment, and the hair
Spread wide upon the grass and daisies fair,

As Love cast down his eyes with a half smile
Godlike and cruel; that faded in a while,
And long he stood above her hidden eyes
With red lips parted in a god's surprise.

CUPID FINDING PSYCHE
ASLEEP IN HER GARDEN

Sir E. Burne-Jones

THE DEFENCE OF GUENEVERE

BUT, knowing now that they would have her speak,
She threw her wet hair backward from her brow,
Her hand close to her mouth touching her cheek,

As though she had had there a shameful blow,
And feeling it shameful to feel ought but shame
All through her heart, yet felt her cheek burned so,

She must a little touch it; like one lame
She walked away from Gauwaine, with her head
Still lifted up; and on her cheek of flame

The tears dried quick; she stopped at last and said:
"O knights and lords, it seems but little skill
To talk of well-known things past now and dead.

"God wot I ought to say, I have done ill,
And pray you all forgiveness heartily!
Because you must be right such great lords—still

"Listen, suppose your time were come to die,
And you were quite alone and very weak;
Yea, laid a dying while very mightily

"The wind was ruffling up the narrow streak
Of river through your broad lands running well:
Suppose a hush should come, then some one speaks:

" 'One of these cloths is heaven, and one is hell,
Now choose one cloth for ever, which they be,
I will not tell you, you must somehow tell

" 'Of your own strength and mightiness; here, see!'
Yea, yea, my lord, and you to ope your eyes,
At foot of your familiar bed to see

"A great God's angel standing, with such dyes,
Not known on earth, on his great wings, and hands,
Held out two ways, light from the inner skies

"Showing him well, and making his commands
Seem to be God's commands, moreover, too,
Holding within his hands the cloths on wands;

"And one of these strange choosing cloths was blue,
Wavy and long and one cut short and red;
No man could tell the better of the two.

"After a shivering half-hour you said,
'God help! heaven's colour, the blue'; and he said, 'hell.'
Perhaps you then would roll upon your bed,

"And cry to all good men that loved you well,
'Ah Christ! if only I had known, known, known';
Launcelot went away, then I could tell,

"Like wisest man how all things would be, moan,
And roll and hurt myself, and long to die,
And yet fear much to die for what was sown.

"Nevertheless you, O Sir Gauwaine, lie,
Whatever may have happened through these years,
God knows I speak truth, saying that you lie."

Her voice was low at first, being full of tears,
But as it cleared, it grew full loud and shrill,
Growing a windy shriek in all men's ears,

A ringing in their startled brains, until
She said that Gauwaine lied, then her voice sunk,
And her great eyes began again to fill,

Though still she stood right up, and never shrunk,
But spoke on bravely, glorious lady fair!
Whatever tears her full lips may have drunk,

She stood, and seemed to think, and wrung her hair,
Spoke out at last with no more trace of shame,
With passionate twisting of her body there:

"It chanced upon a day that Launcelot came
To dwell at Arthur's court: at Christmas-time
This happened; when the heralds sung his name,

" 'Son of King Ban of Benwick,' seemed to chime
Along with all the bells that rang that day,
O'er the white roofs, with little change of rhyme.

"Christmas and whitened winter passed away,
And over me the April sunshine came,
Made very awful with black hail-clouds, yea

"And in the Summer I grew white with flame,
And bowed my head down—Autumn, and the sick
Sure knowledge things would never be the same,

"However often Spring might be most thick
Of blossoms and buds, smote on me, and I grew
Careless of most things, let the clock tick, tick,

"To my unhappy pulse, that beat right through
My eager body; while I laughed out loud,
And let my lips curl up at false or true,

"Seemed cold and shallow without any cloud.
Behold my judges, then the cloths were brought:
While I was dizzied thus, old thoughts would crowd,

"Belonging to the time ere I was bought
By Arthur's great name and his little love;
Must I give up for ever then, I thought,

"That which I deemed would ever round me move
Glorifying all things; for a little word,
Scarce ever meant at all, must I now prove

"Stone-cold for ever? Pray you, does the Lord
Will that all folks should be quite happy and good?
I love God now a little, if this cord

"Were broken, once for all what striving could
Make me love anything in earth or heaven?
So day by day it grew, as if one should

"Slip slowly down some path worn smooth and even,
Down to a cool sea on a summer day;
Yet still in slipping was there some small leaven

"Of stretched hands catching small stones by the way,
Until one surely reached the sea at last,
And felt strange new joy as the worn head lay

"Back, with the hair like sea-weed; yea all past
Sweat of the forehead, dryness of the lips,
Washed utterly out by the dear waves o'ercast

"In the lone sea, far off from any ships!
Do I not know now of a day in Spring?
No minute of that wild day ever slips

"From out my memory; I hear thrushes sing,
And wheresoever I may be, straightway
Thoughts of it all come up with most fresh sting;

"I was half mad with beauty on that day,
And went without my ladies all alone,
In a quiet garden walled round every way;

"I was right joyful of that wall of stone,
That shut the flowers and trees up with the sky,
And trebled all the beauty: to the bone,

"Yea right through to my heart, grown very shy
With weary thoughts, it pierced, and made me glad;
Exceedingly glad, and I knew verily,

"A little thing just then had made me mad;
I dared not think, as I was wont to do,
Sometimes, upon my beauty; if I had

"Held out my long hands up against the blue,
And, looking on the tenderly darken'd fingers,
Thought that by rights one ought to see quite through,

"There, see you, where the soft still light yet lingers,
Round by the edges; what should I have done,
If this had joined with yellow spotted singers,

"And startling green drawn upward by the sun?
But shouting, loosed out, see now! all my hair,
And trancedly stood watching the west wind run

"With faintest half-heard breathing sound—why there
I lose my head e'en now in doing this;
But shortly listen—In that garden fair

"Came Launcelot walking; this is true, the kiss
Wherewith we kissed in meeting that spring day,
I scarce dare talk of the remember'd bliss,

"When both our mouths went wandering in one way,
And aching sorely, met among the leaves;
Our hands being left behind strained far away.

"Never within a yard of my bright sleeves
Had Launcelot come before—and now, so nigh!
After that day why is it Guenevere grieves?

"Nevertheless you, O Sir Gauwaine, lie,
Whatever happened on through all those years,
God knows I speak truth, saying that you lie.

"Being such a lady could I weep these tears
If this were true? A great queen such as I
Having sinn'd this way, straight her conscience sears;

"And afterwards she liveth hatefully,
Slaying and poisoning, certes never weeps—
Gauwaine be friends now speak me lovingly.

"Do I not see how God's dear pity creeps
All through your frame, and trembles in your mouth?
Remember in what grave your mother sleeps,

"Buried in some place far down in the south,
Men are forgetting as I speak to you;
By her head sever'd in that awful drouth

"Of pity that drew Agravaine's fell blow,
I pray your pity! let me not scream out
For ever after, when the shrill winds blow

"Through half your castle-locks! let me not shout
For ever after in the winter night
When you ride out alone! in battle-rout

"Let not my rusting tears make your sword light!
Ah! God of mercy how he turns away!
So, ever must I dress me to the fight,

"So—let God's justice work! Gauwaine, I say,
See me hew down your proofs; yea all men know
Even as you said how Mellyagraunce one day,

"One bitter day in *la Fausse Garde*, for so
All good knights held it after, saw—
Yea, sirs, by cursed unknightly outrage; though

"You, Gauwaine, held his word without a flaw,
This Mellyagraunce saw blood upon my bed—
Whose blood then pray you? is there any law

"To make a queen say why some spots of red
Lie on her coverlet? or will you say,
'Your hands are white, lady, as when you wed,

"'Where did you bleed?' and must I stammer out—'Nay,
I blush indeed, fair lord, only to rend
My sleeve up to my shoulder, where there lay

"'A knife-point last night': so must I defend
The honour of the lady Guenevere?
Not so, fair lords, even if the world should end

"This very day, and you were judges here
Instead of God. Did you see Mellyagraunce
When Launcelot stood by him? what white fear

"Curdled his blood, and how his teeth did dance,
His side sink in? as my knight cried and said,
'Slayer of unarm'd men, here is a chance!

"'Setter of traps, I pray you guard your head,
By God I am so glad to fight with you,
Stripper of ladies, that my hand feels lead

" 'For driving weight; hurrah now! draw and do,
For all my wounds are moving in my breast,
And I am getting mad with waiting so.'

"He struck his hands together o'er the beast,
Who fell down flat, and grovell'd at his feet,
And groan'd at being slain so young—'at least.'

"My knight said, 'Rise you, sir, who are so fleet
At catching ladies, half-arm'd will I fight,
My left side all uncovered!' then I weet,

"Up sprang Sir Mellyagraunce with great delight
Upon his knave's face; not until just then
Did I quite hate him, as I saw my knight

"Along the lists look to my stake and pen
With such a joyous smile, it made me sigh
From agony beneath my waist-chain, when

"The fight began, and to me they drew nigh;
Ever Sir Launcelot kept him on the right,
And traversed warily, and ever high

"And fast leapt caitiff's sword, until my knight
Sudden threw up his sword to his left hand,
Caught it, and swung it; that was all the fight.

"Except a spout of blood on the hot land;
For it was hottest summer; and I know
I wonder'd how the fire, while I should stand,

"And burn, against the heat, would quiver so,
Yards above my head; thus these matters went;
Which things were only warnings of the woe

"That fell on me. Yet Mellyagraunce was shent,
For Mellyagraunce had fought against the Lord;
Therefore, my lords, take heed lest you be blent

"With all this wickedness; say no rash word
Against me, being so beautiful; my eyes,
Wept all away to grey, may bring some sword

"To drown you in your blood; see my breast rise,
Like waves of purple sea, as here I stand;
And how my arms are moved in wonderful wise,

"Yea also at my full heart's strong command,
See through my long throat how the words go up
In ripples to my mouth; how in my hand

"The shadow lies like wine within a cup
Of marvellously colour'd gold; yea now
This little wind is rising, look you up,

"And wonder how the light is falling so
Within my moving tresses: will you dare,
When you have looked a little on my brow,

"To say this thing is vile? or will you care
For any plausible lies of cunning woof,
When you can see my face with no lie there

"For ever? am I not a gracious proof—
'But in your chamber Launcelot was found'—
Is there a good knight then would stand aloof,

"When a queen says with gentle queenly sound:
'O true as steel come now and talk with me,
I love to see your step upon the ground

" 'Unwavering, also well I love to see
That gracious smile light up your face, and hear
Your wonderful words, that all mean verily

" 'The thing they seem to mean; good friend, so dear
To me in everything, come here to-night,
Or else the hours will pass most dull and drear;

" 'If you come not, I fear this time I might
Get thinking over much of times gone by,
When I was young, and green hope was in sight;

" 'For no man cares now to know why I sigh;
And no man comes to sing me pleasant songs,
Nor any brings me the sweet flowers that lie

" 'So thick in the gardens; therefore one so longs
To see you, Launcelot; that we may be
Like children once again, free from all wrongs

" 'Just for one night.' Did he not come to me?
What thing could keep true Launcelot away
If I said 'come'? there was one less than three

"In my quiet room that night, and we were gay;
Till sudden I rose up, weak, pale, and sick,
Because a bawling broke our dream up, yea

"I looked at Launcelot's face and could not speak,
For he looked helpless too, for a little while;
Then I remember now I tried to shriek,

"And could not, but fell down; from tile to tile
The stones they threw up rattled o'er my head,
And made me dizzier; till within a while

"My maids were all about me, and my head
On Launcelot's breast was being soothed away
From its white chattering, until Launcelot said—

"By God! I will not tell you more to-day,
Judge any way you will—what matters it?
You know quite well the story of that fray,

"How Launcelot still'd their bawling, the mad fit
That caught up Gauwaine—all, all, verily,
But just that which would save me; these things flit.

"Nevertheless you, O Sir Gauwaine, lie,
Whatever may have happen'd these long years,
God knows I speak truth, saying that you lie!

"All I have said is truth, by Christ's dear tears."
She would not speak another word, but stood
Turn'd sideways; listening, like a man who hears

His brother's trumpet sounding through the wood
Of his foes' lances. She lean'd eagerly,
And gave a slight spring sometimes, as she could

At last hear something really; joyfully
Her cheek grew crimson, as the headlong speed
Of the roan charger drew all men to see,
The knight who came was Launcelot at good need.

THE HAYSTACK IN THE FLOODS

HAD she come all the way for this,
To part at last without a kiss?
Yea, had she borne the dirt and rain
That her own eyes might see him slain
Beside the haystack in the floods?

Along the dripping leafless woods,
The stirrup touching either shoe,
She rode astride as troopers do;
With kirtle kilted to her knee,
To which the mud splash'd wretchedly;
And the wet dripp'd from every tree
Upon her head and heavy hair,
And on her eyelids broad and fair;
The tears and rain ran down her face.
By fits and starts they rode apace,
And very often was his place
Far off from her; he had to ride
Ahead, to see what might betide
When the roads cross'd; and sometimes, when
There rose a murmuring from his men,
Had to turn back with promises;
Ah me! she had but little ease;
And often for pure doubt and dread
She sobb'd, made giddy in the head
By the swift riding; while, for cold,
Her slender fingers scarce could hold
The wet reins; yea, and scarcely, too,
She felt the foot within her shoe
Against the stirrup: all for this,
To part at last without a kiss
Beside the haystack in the floods.

For when they near'd that old soak'd hay,
They saw across the only way
That Judas, Godmar, and the three
Red running lions dismally
Grinn'd from his pennon, under which,
In one straight line along the ditch,
They counted thirty heads.

JANE BURDEN AS GUINEVERE
D. G. Rossetti

THE BLESSED DAMOZEL
D. G. Rossetti

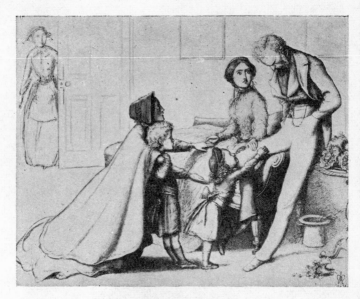

RETRIBUTION
Sir J. E. Millais

PIPPA PASSES
Elizabeth Siddal

So then,
While Robert turn'd round to his men,
She saw at once the wretched end,
And, stooping down, tried hard to rend
Her coif the wrong way from her head,
And hid her eyes; while Robert said:
"Nay, love, 'tis scarcely two to one,
At Poictiers where we made them run
So fast—why, sweet my love, good cheer.
The Gascon frontier is so near,
Nought after this."

            But, "O," she said,
"My God! My God! I have to tread
The long way back without you; then
The court at Paris; those six men;
The gratings of the Chatelet;
The swift Seine on some rainy day
Like this, and people standing by,
And laughing, while my weak hands try
To recollect how strong men swim.
All this, or else a life with him,
For which I should be damned at last.
Would God that this next hour were past!"

He answer'd not, but cried his cry,
"St George for Marny!" cheerily;
And laid his hand upon her rein.
Alas! no man of all his train
Gave back that cheery cry again;
And, while for rage his thumb beat fast
Upon his sword-hilts, some one cast
About his neck a kerchief long,
And bound him.

          Then they went along
To Godmar; who said: "Now, Jehane,
Your lover's life is on the wane
So fast, that, if this very hour
You yield not as my paramour,
He will not see the rain leave off—
Nay, keep your tongue from gibe and scoff,
Sir Robert, or I slay you now."

She laid her hand upon her brow,
Then gazed upon the palm, as though
She thought her forehead bled, and—"No,"
She said, and turn'd her head away,
As there were nothing else to say,
And everything were settled: red
Grew Godmar's face from chin to head:
"Jehane, on yonder hill there stands
My castle, guarding well my lands:
What hinders me from taking you,
And doing that I list to do
To your fair wilful body, while
Your knight lies dead?"

          A wicked smile
Wrinkled her face, her lips grew thin,
A long way out she thrust her chin:
"You know that I should strangle you
While you were sleeping; or bite through
Your throat, by God's help—ah!" she said,
"Lord Jesus, pity your poor maid!

For in such wise they hem me in,
I cannot choose but sin and sin,
Whatever happens; yet I think
They could not make me eat or drink,

And so should I just reach my rest."
"Nay, if you do not my behest,
O Jehane! though I love you well,"
Said Godmar, "would I fail to tell
All that I know." "Foul lies," she said.
"Eh? lies my Jehane? by God's head,
At Paris folks would deem them true!
Do you know, Jehane, they cry for you,
' Jehane the brown! Jehane the brown!
Give us Jehane to burn or drown!'—
Eh—gag me Robert!—sweet my friend,
This were indeed a piteous end
For those long fingers, and long feet,
And long neck, and smooth shoulders sweet;
An end that few men would forget
That saw it—So, an hour yet:
Consider, Jehane, which to take
Of life or death!"

        So, scarce awake,
Dismounting, did she leave that place,
And totter some yards: with her face
Turn'd upward to the sky she lay,
Her head on a wet heap of hay,
And fell asleep; and while she slept,
And did not dream, the minutes crept
Round to the twelve again; but she,
Being waked at last, sigh'd quietly,
And strangely childlike came, and said:
"I will not." Straightway Godmar's head,
As though it hung on strong wires, turn'd
Most sharply round, and his face burn'd.

For Robert—both his eyes were dry,
He could not weep, but gloomily

He seem'd to watch the rain; yea, too,
His lips were firm; he tried once more
To touch her lips; she reach'd out, sore
And vain desire so tortured them,
The poor grey lips, and now the hem
Of his sleeve brush'd them.

        With a start
Up Godmar rose, thrust them apart;
From Robert's throat he loosed the bands
Of silk and mail; with empty hands
Held out, she stood and gazed, and saw,
The long bright blade without a flaw
Glide out from Godmar's sheath, his hand
In Robert's hair; she saw him bend
Back Robert's head; she saw him send
The thin steel down; the blow told well,
Right backward the knight Robert fell,
And moan'd as dogs do, being half dead,
Unwitting, as I deem: so then
Godmar turn'd grinning to his men,
Who ran, some five or six, and beat
His head to pieces at their feet.

Then Godmar turn'd again, and said:
"So, Jehane, the first fitte is read!
Take note, my lady, that your way
Lies backward to the Chatelet!"
She shook her head and gazed awhile
At her cold hands with a rueful smile,
As though this thing had made her mad.

This was the parting that they had
Beside the haystack in the floods.

SHAMEFUL DEATH

THERE were four of us about that bed;
  The mass-priest knelt at the side,
I and his mother stood at the head,
  Over his feet lay the bride;
We were quite sure that he was dead,
  Though his eyes were open wide.

He did not die in the night,
  He did not die in the day,
But in the morning twilight
  His spirit pass'd away,
When neither sun nor moon was bright,
  And the trees were merely grey.

He was not slain with the sword,
  Knight's axe, or the knightly spear,
Yet spoke he never a word
  After he came in here;
I cut away the cord
  From the neck of my brother dear.

He did not strike one blow,
  For the recreants came behind,
In a place where the hornbeams grow,
  A path right hard to find,
For the hornbeam boughs swing so,
  That the twilight makes it blind.

They lighted a great torch then
  When his arms were pinion'd fast,
Sir John the knight of the Fen,
  Sir Guy of the Dolorous Blast,
With knights threescore and ten,
  Hung brave Lord Hugh at last.

I am threescore and ten,
   And my hair is all turn'd grey,
But I met Sir John of the Fen
   Long ago on a summer day,
And am glad to think of the moment when
   I took his life away.

I am threescore and ten,
   And my strength is mostly pass'd,
But long ago I and my men,
   When the sky was overcast,
And the smoke roll'd over the reeds of the fen
   Slew Guy of the Dolorous Blast.

And now, knights all of you,
I pray you pray for Sir Hugh,
A good knight and a true,
And for Alice, his wife, pray too.

Two Red Roses across the Moon

There was a lady lived in a hall,
Large in the eyes, and slim and tall;
And ever she sung from noon to noon,
Two red roses across the moon.

There was a knight came riding by
In early spring, when the roads were dry;
And he heard that lady sing at the noon,
Two red roses across the moon.

Yet none the more he stopp'd at all,
But he rode a-gallop past the hall;
And left that lady singing at noon,
Two red roses across the moon.

CRISEYDE SEES TROILUS RETURN

Sir E. Burne-Jones

Because, forsooth, the battle was set,
And the scarlet and blue had got to be met,
He rode on the spur till the next warm noon—
Two red roses across the moon.

But the battle was scatter'd from hill to hill,
From the windmill to the watermill;
And he said to himself, as it near'd the noon,
Two red roses across the moon.

You scarce could see for the scarlet and blue,
A golden helm or a golden shoe;
So he cried, as the fight grew thick at the noon,
Two red roses across the moon.

Verily then the gold bore through
The huddled spears of the scarlet and blue;
And they cried, as they cut them down at the noon,
Two red roses across the moon.

I trow he stopp'd when he rode again
By the hall, though draggled sore with the rain;
And his lips were pinch'd to kiss at the noon
Two red roses across the moon.

Under the may she stoop'd to the crown,
All was gold, there was nothing of brown;
And the horns blew up in the hall at noon,
Two red roses across the moon.

SUMMER DAWN

PRAY but one prayer for me 'twixt thy closed lips,
  Think but one thought of me up in the stars,
The summer night waneth, the morning light slips,
  Faint and grey 'twixt the leaves of the aspen, betwixt the
     cloud-bars,
  That are patiently waiting there for the dawn;
  Patient and colourless, though Heaven's gold
Waits to float through them along with the sun.
Far out in the meadows, above the young corn,
  The heavy elms wait, and, restless and cold
The uneasy wind rises; the roses are dun;
Through the long twilight they pray for the dawn,
Round the lone house in the midst of the corn.
  Speak but one word to me over the corn,
  Over the tender, bow'd locks of the corn.

The Story of the Unknown Church

I was the master-mason of a church that was built more than six hundred years ago; it is now two hundred years since that church vanished from the face of the earth; it was destroyed utterly—no fragment of it was left; not even the great pillars that bore up the tower at the cross, where the choir used to join the nave. No one knows now even where it stood, only in this very autumn-tide, if you knew the place, you would see the heaps made by the earth-covered ruins heaving the yellow corn into glorious waves, so that the place where my church used to be is as beautiful now as when it stood in all its splendour. I do not remember very much about the land where my church was; I have quite forgotten the name of it, but I know it was very beautiful, and even now, while I am thinking of it, comes a flood of old memories, and I almost seem to see it again—that old beautiful land! only dimly do I see it in spring and summer and winter, but I see it in autumn-tide clearly now; yes, clearer, clearer, oh! so bright and glorious! yet it was beautiful too in spring, when the brown earth began to grow green: beautiful in summer, when the blue sky looked so much bluer, if you could hem a piece of it in between the new white carving; beautiful in the solemn starry nights, so solemn that it almost reached agony—the awe and joy one had in their great beauty. But of all these beautiful times, I remember the whole only of autumn-tide; the others come in bits to me; I can think only of parts of them, but all of autumn; and of all days and nights in autumn, I remember one more particularly. That autumn day the church was nearly finished, and the monks, for whom we were building the church, and the people, who lived in the town hard by, crowded round us oftentimes to watch us carving.

Now the great Church, and the buildings of the Abbey where the monks lived, were about three miles from the town, and the town stood on a hill overlooking the rich autumn country;

it was girt about with great walls that had overhanging battle-ments, and towers at certain places all along the walls, and often we could see from the churchyard or the Abbey garden, the flash of helmets and spears, and the dim shadowy waving of banners, as the knights and lords and men-at-arms passed to and fro along the battlements; and we could see too in the town the three spires of the three churches; and the spire of the Cathedral, which was the tallest of the three, was gilt all over with gold, and always at night-time a great lamp shone from it that hung in the spire midway between the roof of the church and the cross at the top of the spire. The Abbey where we built the Church was not girt by stone walls, but by a circle of poplar trees, and whenever a wind passed over them, were it ever so little a breath, it set them all a-ripple; and when the wind was high, they bowed and swayed very low, and the wind, as it lifted the leaves, and showed their silvery white sides, or as again in the lulls of it, it let them drop, kept on changing the trees from green to white, and white to green; moreover, through the boughs and trunks of the poplars, we caught glimpses of the great golden corn sea, waving, waving, waving for leagues and leagues; and among the corn grew burning scarlet poppies, and blue corn-flowers; and the corn-flowers were so blue, that they gleamed, and seemed to burn with a steady light, as they grew beside the poppies among the gold of the wheat. Through the corn sea ran a blue river, and always green meadows and lines of tall poplars followed its windings. The old Church had been burned, and that was the reason why the monks caused me to build the new one; the buildings of the Abbey were built at the same time as the burned-down Church, more than a hundred years before I was born, and they were on the north side of the Church, and joined to it by a cloister of round arches, and in the midst of the cloister was a lawn, and in the midst of that lawn, a fountain of marble, carved round about with flowers and strange beasts; and at the edge of the lawn, near the round arches, were a great many sun-flowers that were all in blossom on that autumn day; and up many of the pillars of the cloister crept passion-flowers and roses. Then, farther from the Church, and past the cloister and its buildings, were many detached buildings, and a great garden round them, all within the circle of the poplar trees; in the garden were trellises covered over with roses, and convolvulus, and the great-leaved fiery nasturtium; and specially all along by the poplar trees were there trellises, but on these grew nothing but deep crimson roses; the hollyhocks too were all out in blossom at that time, great spires of pink, and orange, and red, and white, with their soft, downy leaves. I said that nothing grew on the trellises by the poplars but crimson roses, but I was not quite right, for in many places the wild flowers had crept into the garden from without; lush green briony, with green-white blossoms, that grows so fast, one could almost think that we see it grow, and deadly nightshade, La bella donna, O! so beautiful; red berry and purple, yellow-spiked flower, and deadly, cruel-looking, dark green leaf, all growing together in the glorious days of early autumn. And in the midst of the great garden was a conduit, with its sides carved with histories from the Bible, and there was on it too, as on the fountain in the cloister, much carving of flowers and strange beasts. Now the Church itself was surrounded on every side but the north by the cemetery, and there were many graves there, both of monks and of laymen, and often the friends of those, whose bodies lay there, had planted flowers about the graves of those they loved. I remember one such particularly, for at the head of it was a cross of carved wood, and at the foot of it, facing the cross, three tall sun-flowers; then in the midst of the cemetery was a cross of stone, carved on one side with the Crucifixion of our Lord Jesus Christ, and on the other with Our Lady holding the Divine Child. So that day, that I specially remember, in Autumn-tide, when the church was nearly finished, I was carving in the central porch of the west front; (for I carved all those bas-reliefs in the west front with my own hand;) beneath me my sister Margaret was carving at the flower-work, and the little quatrefoils that carry the signs of the zodiac and emblems of the months; now my sister Margaret was rather more than twenty years old at that time, and she was very beautiful, with dark brown hair and deep calm violet eyes. I had lived with her all my life, lived with her almost alone latterly, for our father and mother died when she was quite young, and I loved her very much, though I was not thinking of her just then, as she stood beneath me carving. Now the central porch was carved with a bas-relief of the Last Judgement, and it was divided into three parts by horizontal bands of deep flower-work. In the lowest division, just over the doors, was carved The Rising of the Dead; above were angels blowing long trumpets, and Michael the Archangel weighing the souls, and the blessed led into heaven by angels, and the lost into hell by the devil; and in the topmost division was the Judge of the world.

All the figures in the porch were finished except one, and I remember when I woke that morning my exultation at the thought of my Church being so nearly finished; I remember, too, how a kind of misgiving mingled with the exultation, which, try all I could, I was unable to shake off; I thought then it was a rebuke for my pride, well, perhaps it was. The figure I had to carve was Abraham, sitting with a blossoming tree on each side of him, holding in his two hands the corners of his great robe, so that it made a mighty fold wherein, with their hands crossed over their breasts, were the souls of the faithful, of whom he was called Father; I stood on the scaffolding for some time, while Margaret's chisel worked on bravely down below. I took mine in my hand, and stood so, listening to the noise of the masons inside, and two monks of the Abbey came and stood below me, and a knight, holding his little daughter by the hand, who every now and then looked up at him, and asked him strange questions. I did not think of these long, but began to think of Abraham, yet I could not think of him sitting there, quiet and solemn, while the Judgement-Trumpet was being blown; I rather thought of him as he looked when he chased those kings so far: riding far ahead of any of his company, with his mail-hood off his head, and lying in grim folds down his back, with the strong west wind blowing his wild black hair far out behind him, with the wind rippling the long scarlet pennon of his lance; riding there amid the rocks and the sands alone; with the last gleam of the armour of the beaten kings disappearing behind the winding of the pass; with his company a long, long way behind, quite out of sight, though their trumpets sounded faintly among the clefts of the rocks: and so I thought I saw him, till in his fierce chase he leapt, horse and man, into a deep river, quiet, swift, and smooth; and there was something in the moving of the water-lilies as the breast of the horse swept them aside, that suddenly took away the thought of Abraham and brought a strange dream of lands I had never seen; and the first was of a place where I was quite alone, standing by the side of a river, and there was the sound of singing a very long way off, but no living thing of any kind could be seen, and the land was quite flat, quite without hills, and quite without trees too, and the river wound very much, making all kinds of quaint curves, and on the side where I stood there grew nothing but long grass, but on the other side grew, quite on to the horizon, a great sea of red corn-poppies, only paths of white lilies wound all among them, with here and there a great golden sun-flower. So I looked down at the river by my feet, and saw how blue it was, and how, as the stream went swiftly by, it swayed to and fro the long green weeds, and I stood and looked at the river for long, till at last I felt some one touch me on the shoulder, and, looking round, I saw standing by me my friend Amyot, whom I love better than any one else in the world, but I thought in my dream that I was frightened when I saw him, for his face had changed so, it was so bright and almost transparent, and his eyes gleamed and shone as I had never seen them do before. Oh! he was so wondrously beautiful, so fearfully beautiful! and as I looked at him the distant music swelled, and seemed to come close up to me, and then swept by us, and fainted away, at last died off entirely; and then I felt sick at heart, and faint, and parched, and I stooped to drink of the water of the river, and as soon as the water touched my lips, lo! the river vanished, and the flat country with its poppies and lilies, and I dreamed that I was in a boat by myself again, floating in an almost land-locked bay of the northern sea, under a cliff of dark basalt. I was lying on my back in the boat, looking up at the intensely blue sky, and a long low swell from the outer sea lifted the boat up and let it fall again and carried it gradually nearer and nearer towards the dark cliff; and as I moved on, I saw at last, on the top of the cliff, a castle, with many towers, and on the highest tower of the castle there was a great white banner floating, with a red chevron on it, and three golden stars on the chevron; presently I saw too on one of the towers, growing in a cranny of the worn stones, a great bunch of golden and blood-red wall-flowers, and I watched the wall-flowers and banner for long; when suddenly I heard a trumpet blow from the castle, and saw a rush of armed men on to the battlements, and there was a fierce fight, till at last it was ended, and one went to the banner and pulled it down, and cast it over the cliff into the sea, and it came down in long sweeps, with the wind making little ripples in it; slowly, slowly it came, till at last it fell over me and covered me from my feet till over my breast, and I let it stay there and looked again at the castle, and then I saw that there was an amber-coloured banner floating over the castle in place of the red chevron and it was much larger than the other; also now, a man stood on the battlements, looking towards me; he had a tilting helmet on, with the visor down, and an amber-coloured surcoat over his armour; his right hand was ungauntleted, and he held it high above his head, and in his hand was the bunch of wall-flowers that I had seen growing on the wall; and his hand was white and small, like a woman's, for in my dream I could see even very far off things much clearer than we see real material things on the earth: presently he threw the wall-flowers over the cliff, and they fell in the boat just behind my head, and then I saw, looking down from the battlements of the castle, Amyot. He looked down towards me very sorrowfully, I thought, but, even as in the other dream, said nothing; so I thought in my dream that I wept for very pity, and for love of him, for he looked as a man just risen from a long illness, and who will carry till he dies a dull pain about with him. He was very thin, and his long black hair drooped all about his face, as he leaned over the battlements looking at me: he was quite pale, and his cheeks were hollow, but his eyes large, and soft, and sad. So I reached out my arms to him, and suddenly I was walking with him in a lovely garden, and we said nothing, for the music which I had heard at first was sounding close to us now, and there were many birds in the boughs of the trees: oh, such birds! gold and ruby, and emerald, but they sung not at all, but were quite silent, as though they too were listening to the music. Now all this time Amyot and I had been looking at each other, but just then I turned my head away from him, and as soon as I did so, the music ended with a long wail, and when I turned again Amyot was gone; then I felt even more sad and sick at heart than I had before when I was by the river, and I leaned against a tree, and put my hands before my eyes. When I looked again the garden was gone, and I knew not where I was, and presently all my dreams were gone. The chips were flying bravely from the stone under my chisel at last, and all my thoughts now were in my carving, when I heard my name, "Walter," called, and when I looked down I saw one standing below me, whom I had seen in my dreams just before— Amyot. I had no hopes of seeing him for a long time, perhaps I might never see him again, I thought, for he was away (as I thought) fighting in the holy wars, and it made me almost beside myself to see him standing close by me in the flesh. I got down from my scaffolding as soon as I could, and all thoughts else were soon drowned in the joy of having him by me; Margaret, too, how glad she must have been, for she had been betrothed to him for some time before he went to the wars, and he had been five years away; five years! and how we had thought of him through those many weary days! how often his face had come before me! his brave, honest face, the most beautiful among all the faces of men and women I have ever seen. Yes, I remember how five years ago I held his hand as we came together out of the cathedral of that great, far-off city, whose name I forget now; and then I remember the stamping of the horses' feet; I remember how his hand left mine at last, and then, some one looking back at me earnestly as they all rode on together—looking back, with his hand on the saddle behind him, while the trumpets sang in long solemn peals as they all rode on together, with the glimmer of arms and the fluttering of banners, and the clinking of the rings of the mail, that sounded like the falling of many drops of water into the deep, still waters of some pool that the rocks nearly meet over; and the gleam and flash of the swords, and the glimmer of the lance-heads and the flutter of the rippled banners, that streamed out from them, swept past me, and were gone, and they seemed like a pageant in a dream, whose meaning we know not; and those sounds too, the trumpets, and the clink of the mail, and the thunder of the horse-hoofs, they seemed dream-like too— and it was all like a dream that he should leave me, for we had said that we should always be together; but he went away, and now he is come back again.

We were by his bed-side, Margaret and I; I stood and leaned over him, and my hair fell sideways over my face and touched his face: Margaret kneeled beside me, quivering in every limb, not with pain, I think, but rather shaken by a passion of earnest prayer. After some time (I know not how long), I looked up from his face to the window underneath which he lay; I do not

LAUNCELOT IN THE QUEEN'S CHAMBER

D. G. Rossetti

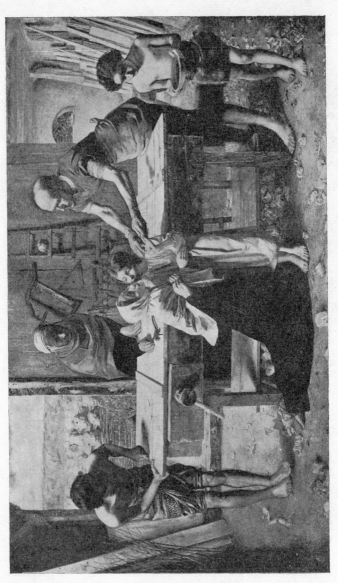

CHRIST IN THE HOUSE OF HIS PARENTS

Sir J. E. Millais

know what time of the day it was, but I know that it was a glorious autumn day, a day soft with melting golden haze: a vine and a rose grew together, and trailed half across the window, so that I could not see much of the beautiful blue sky, and nothing of town or country beyond; the vine leaves were touched with red here and there, and three over-blown roses, light pink roses, hung amongst them. I remember dwelling on the strange lines the autumn had made in red on one of the gold-green vine leaves, and watching one leaf of one of the over-blown roses, expecting it to fall every minute; but as I gazed, and felt disappointed that the rose leaf had not fallen yet, I felt my pain suddenly shoot through me, and I remembered what I had lost; and then came bitter, bitter dreams—dreams which had once made me happy—dreams of the things I had hoped would be, of the things that would never be now; they came between the fair vine leaves and rose blossoms, and that which lay before the window; they came as before, perfect in colour and form, sweet sounds and shapes. But now in every one was something unutterably miserable; they would not go away, they put out the steady glow of the golden haze, the sweet light of the sun through the vine leaves, the soft leaning of the full blown roses. I wandered in them for a long time; at last I felt a hand put me aside gently, for I was standing at the head of—of the bed; then some one kissed my forehead, and words were spoken—I know not what words. The bitter dreams left me for the bitterer reality at last; for I had found him that morning lying dead, only the morning after I had seen him when he had come back from his long absence—I had found him lying dead, with his hands crossed downwards, with his eyes closed, as though the angels had done that for him; and now when I looked at him he still lay there, and Margaret knelt by him with her face touching his: she was not quivering now, her lips moved not at all as they had done just before; and so, suddenly those words came to my mind which she had spoken when she kissed me, and which at the time I had only heard with my outward hearing, for she had said, "Walter, farewell, and Christ keep you; but for me, I must be with him, for so I promised him last night that I would never leave him any more, and God will let me go." And verily Margaret and Amyot did go, and left me very lonely and sad.

It was just beneath the westernmost arch of the nave, there I carved their tomb. I was a long time carving it; I did not think I should be so long at first, and I said, "I shall die when I have finished carving it," thinking that would be a very short time. But so it happened after I had carved those two whom I loved, lying with clasped hands like husband and wife above their tomb, that I could not yet leave carving it; and so that I might be near them I became a monk, and used to sit in the choir and sing, thinking of the time when we should all be together again. And as I had time I used to go to the westernmost arch of the nave and work at the tomb that was there under the great, sweeping arch; and in process of time I raised a marble canopy that reached quite up to the top of the arch, and I pointed it too as fair as I could, and carved it all about with many flowers and histories, and in them I carved the faces of those I had known on earth (for I was not as one on earth now, but seemed quite away out of the world). And as I carved, sometimes the monks and other people too would come and gaze, and watch how the flowers grew; and sometimes too as they gazed, they would weep for pity, knowing how all had been. So my life passed, and I lived in that abbey for twenty years after he died, till one morning, quite early, when they came into the church for matins, they found me lying dead, with my chisel in my hand, underneath the last lily of the tomb.

From "The Story of the Glittering Plain"

[*Hallblithe, whose betrothed has been carried off by sea-raiders, has gone in search of her and has reached the Isle of Ransom. Here he meets a bed-ridden old man who, promising to help him, advises him to answer any challenge only with the words, " The House of the Un- dying."*]

So Hallblithe went back into the main hall, and the sun had gotten round now, and was shining into the hall through the clerestory windows, so that he saw clearly all that was therein. And he deemed the hall fairer within than without; and especially over the shut-beds were many stories carven in the panelling, and Hallblithe beheld them gladly. But of one thing he marvelled, that whereas he was in an island of the strong-thieves of the waters, and in their very home and chiefest habitation, there were no ships or seas pictured in that imagery, but fair groves and gardens, with flowery grass and fruited trees all about. And there were fair women abiding therein, and lovely young men, and warriors, and strange beasts and many marvels, and the ending of wrath and beginning of pleasure, and the crowning of love. And amidst these was pictured oft and again a mighty king with a sword by his side and a crown on his head; and ever was he smiling and joyous, so that Hallblithe, when he looked on him, felt of better heart and smiled back on the carven image.

So while Hallblithe looked on these things, and pondered his case carefully, all alone as he was in that alien hall, he heard a noise without of talking and laughter, and presently the pattering of feet therewith, and then women came into the hall, a score or more, some young, some old, some fair enough, and some hard-featured and uncomely, but all above the stature of the women whom he had seen in his own land.

So he stood amidst the hall-floor and abided them; and they saw him and his shining war-gear, and ceased their talking and laughter, and drew round about him, and gazed at him; but none said aught till an old crone came forth from the ring, and said: "Who art thou, standing under weapons in our hall?"

He knew not what to answer, and held his peace; and she spake again: "Whither wouldest thou, what seekest thou?"

Then answered Hallblithe: "*The House of the Undying.*"

None answered, and the other women all fell away from him at once, and went about their business hither and thither through the hall. But the old crone took him by the hand, and led him up to the dais, and set him next to the midmost high-seat. Then she made as if she would do off his war-gear, and he would not gainsay her, though he deemed that foes might be anear; for in sooth he trusted in the old carle that he would not betray him, and moreover he deemed it would be unmanly not to take the risks of the guesting, according to the custom of that country.

So she took his armour and his weapons and bore them off to a shut-bed next to that wherein lay the ancient man, and she laid the gear within it, all save the spear, which she laid on the wall-pins above; and she made signs to him that therein he was to lie; but she spake no word to him. Then she brought him the hand-washing water in a basin of latten, and a goodly towel therewith, and when he had washed she went away from him, but not far.

This while the other women were busy about the hall; some swept the floor down, and when it was swept strawed thereon rushes and handfuls of wild thyme: some went into the buttery and bore forth the boards and the trestles: some went to the chests and brought out the rich hangings, the goodly bankers and dorsars, and did them on the walls; some bore in the stoups and horns and beakers, and some went their ways and came not back awhile, for they were busied about the cooking. But whatever they did, none hailed him, or heeded him more than if he had been an image, as he sat there looking on. None save the old woman who brought him the fore-supper, to wit a great horn of mead, and cakes and dried fish.

So was the hall arrayed for the feast very fairly, and Hall-blithe sat there while the sun westered and the house grew dim, and dark at last, and they lighted the candles up and down the hall. But a little after these were lit, a great horn was winded close without, and thereafter came the clatter of arms about the door, and exceeding tall weaponed men came in, one score and five, and strode two by two up to the foot of the dais, and stood there in a row. And Hallblithe deemed their war-gear exceeding good; they were all clad in ring-locked byrnies, and had steel helms on their heads with garlands of gold wrought about them and they bore spears in their hands, and white shields hung at their backs. Now came the women to them and unarmed them; and under their armour their raiment was black; but they had gold rings on their arms, and golden collars about their necks. So they strode up to the dais and took their places on the high-seat, not heeding Hallblithe any more than if he were an image of wood. Nevertheless that man sat next to him who was the chieftain of all and sat in the midmost high-seat; and he bore his sheathed sword in his hand and laid it on the board before him, and he was the only man of those chieftains who had a weapon.

ALGERNON CHARLES SWINBURNE

A Ballad of Death

Kneel down, fair Love, and fill thyself with tears,
Girdle thyself with sighing for a girth
Upon the sides of mirth,
Cover thy lips and eyelids, let thine ears
Be filled with rumour of people sorrowing;
Make thee soft raiment out of woven sighs
Upon the flesh to cleave,
Set pains therein and many a grievous thing,

And many sorrows after each his wise
For armlet and for gorget and for sleeve.

O Love's lute heard about the lands of death,
Left hanged upon the trees that were therein;
O Love and Time and Sin,
Three singing mouths that mourn now under breath,
Three lovers, each one evil spoken of;
O smitten lips where through this voice of mine
Came softer with her praise;
Abide a little for our lady's love.
The kisses of her mouth were more than wine,
And more than peace the passage of her days.

O Love, thou knowest if she were good to see.
O Time, thou shalt not find in any land
Till, cast out of thine hand,
The sunlight and the moonlight fail from thee,
Another woman fashioned like as this.
O Sin, thou knowest that all thy shame in her
Was made a goodly thing;
Yea, she caught Shame and shamed him with her kiss,
With her fair kiss, and lips much lovelier
Than lips of amorous roses in late spring.

By night there stood over against my bed
Queen Venus with a hood striped gold and black,
Both sides drawn fully back
From brows wherein the sad blood failed of red,
And temples drained of purple and full of death.
Her curled hair had the wave of sea-water
And the sea's gold in it.
Her eyes were as a dove's that sickeneth.
Strewn dust of gold she had shed over her,
And pearl and purple and amber on her feet.

Upon her raiment of dyed sendaline
Were painted all the secret ways of love
And covered things thereof,
That hold delight as grape-flowers hold their wine;
Red mouths of maidens and red feet of doves,
And brides that kept within the bride-chamber
Their garment of soft shame,
And weeping faces of the wearied loves
That swoon in sleep and awake wearier,
With heat of lips and hair shed out like flame.

The tears that through her eyelids fell on me
Made mine own bitter where they ran between
As blood had fallen therein,
She saying; Arise, lift up thine eyes and see
If any glad thing be or any good
Now the best thing is taken forth of us;
Even she to whom all praise
Was as one flower in a great multitude,
One glorious flower of many and glorious,
One day found gracious among many days:

Even she whose handmaiden was Love—to whom
At kissing times across her stateliest bed
Kings bowed themselves and shed
Pale wine, and honey with the honeycomb,
And spikenard bruised for a burnt-offering;
Even she between whose lips the kiss became
As fire and frankincense;
Whose hair was as gold raiment on a king,
Whose eyes were as the morning purged with flame,
Whose eyelids as sweet savour issuing thence.

Then I beheld, and lo on the other side
My lady's likeness crowned and robed and dead.

Sweet still, but now not red,
Was the shut mouth whereby men lived and died.
And sweet, but emptied of the blood's blue shade,
The great curled eyelids that withheld her eyes.
And sweet, but like spoilt gold,
The weight of colour in her tresses weighed.
And sweet, but as a vesture with new dyes,
The body that was clothed with love of old.

Ah! that my tears filled all her woven hair
And all the hollow bosom of her gown—
Ah! that my tears ran down
Even to the place where many kisses were,
Even where her parted breast-flowers have place,
Even where they are cloven apart—who known not this?
Ah! the flowers cleave apart
And their sweet fills the tender interspace;
Ah! the leaves grown thereof were things to kiss
Ere their fine gold was tarnished at the heart.

Ah! in the days when God did good to me,
Each part about her was a righteous thing;
Her mouth an almsgiving,
The glory of her garments charity,
The beauty of her bosom a good deed,
In the good days when God kept sight of us;
Love lay upon her eyes,
And on that hair whereof the world takes heed:
And all her body was more virtuous
Than souls of women fashioned otherwise.

Now, ballad, gather poppies in thine hands
And sheaves of brier and many rusted sheaves
Rain-rotten in rank lands,
Waste marigold and late unhappy leaves

And grass that fades ere any of it be mown;
And when thy bosom is filled full thereof
Seek out Death's face ere the light altereth,
And say "My master that was thrall to Love
Is become thrall to Death."
Bow down before him, ballad, sigh and groan,
But make no sojourn in thy outgoing;
For haply it may be
That when thy feet return at evening
Death shall come in with thee.

THE KING'S DAUGHTER

WE were ten maidens in the green corn,
 Small red leaves in the mill-water:
Fairer maidens never were born,
 Apples of gold for the king's daughter.

We were ten maidens by a well-head,
 Small white birds in the mill-water;
Sweeter maidens never were wed,
 Rings of red for the king's daughter.

The first to spin, the second to sing,
 Seeds of wheat in the mill-water;
The third may was a goodly thing,
 White bread and brown for the king's daughter.

The fourth to sew and the fifth to play,
 Fair green weed in the mill-water;
The sixth may was a goodly may,
 White wine and red for the king's daughter.

The seventh to woo, the eighth to wed,
　　Fair thin weeds in the mill-water;
The ninth had gold work on her head,
　　Honey in the comb for the king's daughter.

The ninth had gold work round her hair,
　　Fallen flowers in the mill-water;
The tenth may was goodly and fair,
　　Golden gloves for the king's daughter.

We were ten maidens in a field green,
　　Fallen fruit in the mill-water;
Fairer maidens never have been,
　　Golden sleeves for the king's daughter.

By there comes the king's young son,
　　A little wind in the mill-water;
"Out of ten maidens ye'll grant me one,"
　　A crown of red for the king's daughter.

"Out of ten mays ye'll give me the best,"
　　A little rain in the mill-water;
A bed of yellow straw for all the rest,
　　A bed of gold for the king's daughter.

He's ta'en out the goodliest,
　　Rain that rains in the mill-water;
A comb of yellow shell for all the rest,
　　A comb of gold for the king's daughter.

He's made her bed to the goodliest,
　　Wind and hail in the mill-water;
A grass girdle for all the rest,
　　A girdle of arms for the king's daughter.

He's set his heart to the goodliest,
　　Snow that snows in the mill-water;
Nine little kisses for all the rest,
　　An hundredfold for the king's daughter.

He's ta'en his leave at the goodliest,
　　Broken boats in the mill-water;
Golden gifts for all the rest,
　　Sorrow of heart for the king's daughter.

"Ye'll make a grave for my fair body,"
　　Running rain in the mill-water;
"And ye'll streek my brother at the side of me,"
　　The pains of hell for the king's daughter.

The Sundew

A little marsh-plant, yellow green,
And pricked at lip with tender red.
Tread close, and either way you tread
Some faint black water jets between
Lest you should bruise the curious head.

A live thing maybe; who shall know?
The summer knows and suffers it;
For the cool moss is thick and sweet
Each side, and saves the blossom so
That it lives out the long June heat.

The deep scent of the heather burns
About it; breathless though it be,
Bow down and worship; more than we
Is the least flower whose life returns,
Least weed renascent in the sea.

We are vexed and cumbered in earth's sight
With wants, with many memories;
These see their mother what she is,
Glad-growing, till August leave more bright
The apple-coloured cranberries.

Wind blows and bleaches the strong grass,
Blown all one way to shelter it
From trample of strayed kine, with feet
Felt heavier than the moorhen was,
Strayed up past patches of wild wheat.

PSYCHE WADING
ACROSS THE STREAM

Sir E. Burne-Jones

You call it sundew; how it grows,
If with its colour it have breath,
If life taste sweet to it, if death
Pain its soft petal, no man knows:
Man has no sight or sense that saith.

My sundew, grown of gentle days,
In these green miles the spring begun
Thy growth ere April had half done
With the soft secret of her ways
Or June made ready for the sun.

O red-lipped mouth of marsh-flower,
I have a secret halved with thee.
The name that is love's name to me
Thou knowest, and the face of her
Who is my festival to see.

The hard sun, as thy petals knew,
Coloured the heavy moss-water:
Thou wert not worth green midsummer
Nor fit to live to August blue,
O sundew, not remembering her.

THE CONTEMPORARY VIEW OF
PRE-RAPHAELITISM

CHARLES DICKENS

A CRITICISM OF MILLAIS' "CHRIST IN THE HOUSE OF HIS PARENTS"

You come—in this Royal Academy Exhibition, which is familiar with the works of Wilkie, Collins, Etty, Eastlake, Leslie, Maclise, Turner, Stanfield, Landseer, Roberts, Danby, Creswick, Lee, Webster, Herbert, Dyce, Cope, and others who would have been renowned as great masters in any age or country—you come, in this place, to the contemplation of a Holy Family. You will have the goodness to discharge from your minds all Post-Raphael ideas, all religious aspirations, all elevating thoughts; all tender, awful, sorrowful, ennobling, sacred, graceful, or beautiful associations; and to prepare yourselves, as befits such a subject—Pre-Raphaelly considered—for the lowest depths of what is mean, odious, repulsive, and revolting.

You behold the interior of a carpenter's shop. In the foreground of that carpenter's shop is a hideous, wry-necked, blubbering, red-headed boy, in a bed-gown; who appears to have received a poke in the hand, from the stick of another boy with whom he has been playing in an adjacent gutter, and to be holding it up for the contemplation of a kneeling woman, so horrible in her ugliness, that (supposing it were possible for any human creature to exist for a moment with that dislocated throat) she would stand out from the rest of the company as a Monster, in the vilest cabaret in France, or the lowest gin-shop in England. Two almost naked carpenters, master and journeyman, worthy companions of the agreeable female, are working at their trade; a boy, with some small flavour of humanity in him, is entering with a vessel of water; and nobody is paying any attention to a snuffy old woman who seems to have mistaken that shop for the tobacconist's next door, and to be hopelessly waiting at the counter to be served with half an ounce of her favourite mixture. Wherever it is possible to express ugliness of feature, limb, or attitude, you have it expressed. Such men as the carpenters might be undressed in any hospital where dirty drunkards, in a high state of varicose veins, are received. Their very toes have walked out of St Giles's.

ANONYMOUS

FROM A REVIEW OF "THE DEFENCE OF GUENEVERE AND OTHER POEMS" IN "THE ATHENAEUM" (April 3, 1858)

DISPOSED as we are, to recognize all who cultivate poetry honestly, whatever be the style—and admitting that Mr Morris may be counted among that choir—we must call attention to his book of Pre-Raphaelite minstrelsy as a curiosity which shows how far affectation may mislead an earnest man towards the fog-land of Art. Of course in the rejoinder, we may be reminded how Wordsworth was misunderstood, how Keats was misprized, when they set forth on their original paths. We shall once more be invited to accept, wrapped round with some delicate roseleaf of sophistry, or locked up in some casket of curious device the fallacy that—

Naught is everything, and everything is naught.

—What matter? Truth is the same, poetry undying from all time and in all ages; but masquing is not truth and the galvanism of old legend is not poetry. The justice of what has been said could be proved from every page of this provoking volume to the satisfaction of the most enthusiastic lover of our laureate's *Lady of Shalott*. That strange dream, which, however beautiful, quaint and touching it be, quivers on the furthest verge of Dream-land to which sane fancy can penetrate, has been the point of departure of Mr Morris.

ROBERT BUCHANAN and *DANTE GABRIEL ROSSETTI*

The most severe and the most influential attack on Pre-Raphaelite poetry was that published by Robert Buchanan under the pseudonym "Thomas Maitland" in "The Contemporary Review" of October 1871. His title was arresting and provocative, and the work earned a speedy notoriety. Its lively journalistic manner and its exaggerations have obscured its critical value, but the following abridgement of it shows some truth in his charges.

FROM "THE FLESHLY SCHOOL OF POETRY: MR D. G. ROSSETTI"

[*Buchanan begins by assigning to contemporary poets roles in "Hamlet". Tennyson is the Prince, though Browning "may be said, however, to play the leading character in his own peculiar fashion on alternate nights." Arnold is Horatio, Buchanan himself Cornelius. Swinburne and Morris become Rosencrantz and Guildenstern, and the part of Osric is reserved for Rossetti.*

He sees Pre-Raphaelite poetry as stemming from Tennyson, its sensualism from "Vivien" and its "hysteric tone and overloaded style" from "Maud," but these poets are deficient in "moral or intellectual quality to temper and control" their fleshliness. Accusing them of being a "Mutual Admiration School," he proposes confining his attention to Rossetti.]

Mr Rossetti has been known for many years as a painter of exceptional powers, who, for reasons best known to himself, has shrunk from publicly exhibiting his pictures, and from allowing anything like a popular estimate to be formed of their qualities. He belongs, or is said to belong, to the so-called Pre-Raphaelite school, a school which is generally considered to exhibit much genius for colour, and great indifference to perspective. It would be unfair to judge the painter by the glimpses we have had of his works, or by the photographs which are sold of the principal paintings. Judged by the photographs he is an artist who conceives unpleasantly, and draws ill. Like Mr Simeon Solomon, however, with whom he seems to have many points in common, he is distinctively a colourist, and of his capabilities in colour we cannot speak, though we should guess that they are great; for if there is any good quality by which his poems are specially marked, it is a great sensitiveness to hues and tints as conveyed in poetic epithet. These qualities, which impress the casual spectator of the photographs from his pictures, are to be found abundantly among his verses. There is the same thinness and transparence of design, the same combination of the simple and the grotesque, the same morbid deviation from healthy forms of life, the same sense of weary, wasting, yet exquisite sensuality; nothing virile, nothing tender, nothing completely sane; a superfluity of extreme sensibility, of delight in beautiful forms, hues and tints, and a deep-seated indifference to all agitating forces and agencies, all tumultuous griefs and sorrows, all the thunderous stress of life, and all the straining storm of speculation. Mr Morris is often pure, fresh and wholesome as his own great model; Mr Swinburne startles us more than once by some fine flash of insight; but the mind of Mr Rossetti is like a glassy mere, broken only by the dive of some water-bird, or the hum of winged insects, and brooded over by an atmosphere of insufferable closeness, with a light blue sky above it, sultry depths mirrored within it, and a surface so thickly sown with water-lilies that it retains its glassy smoothness even in the strongest wind. Judged relatively to his poetic associates,

Mr Rossetti must be pronounced inferior to either. He cannot tell a pleasant story like Mr Morris, nor forge alliterative thunderbolts like Mr Swinburne. It must be conceded, nevertheless, that he is neither so glibly imitative as the one, nor so transcendentally superficial as the other.

Although he has been known for many years as a poet as well as a painter—as a painter and poet idolized by his own family and personal associates—and although he has once or twice appeared in print as a contributor to magazines, Mr Rossetti did not formally appeal to the public until rather more than a year ago, when he published a copious volume of poems, with the announcement that the book, although it contained pieces composed at intervals during a period of many years, "included nothing which the author believes to be immature." This work was inscribed to his brother, Mr William Rossetti, who, having written much both in poetry and criticism, will perhaps be known to bibliographers as the editor of the worst edition of Shelley which has yet seen the light. No sooner had the work appeared than the chorus of eulogy began. "The book is satisfactory from end to end," wrote Mr Morris in the *Academy*; "I think these lyrics, with all their other merits, the most complete of their time; nor do I know what lyrics of any time are to be called *great*, if we are to deny the title to these." On the same subject Mr Swinburne went into a hysteria of admiration: "golden affluence," "jewel-coloured words," "chastity of form," "harmonious nakedness," "consummate fleshly sculpture," and so on in Mr Swinburne's well known manner when reviewing his friends. Other critics with a singular similarity of phrase, followed suit. Strange to say, moreover, no one accused Mr Rossetti of naughtiness. What had been heinous in Mr Swinburne was majestic exquisiteness in Mr Rossetti. Yet we question if there is anything in the unfortunate *Poems and Ballads* quite so questionable on the score of thorough nastiness as many pieces in Mr Rossetti's collection. Mr Swinburne was wilder, more outrageous, more blasphemous, and his subjects were more atrocious in themselves; yet the hysterical tone slew the animalism, the furiousness of epithet lowered the sensation; and the first feeling of disgust at such themes as *Laus Veneris* and *Anactoria* faded away into comic amazement. It was only a little mad boy letting off squibs; not a great strong man, who might be really dangerous to society. "I *will* be naughty!" screamed the little boy; but, after all, what did it matter? It is quite different, however, when a grown man, with the self-control and easy audacity of actual experience, comes forward to chronicle his amorous sensations, and, first proclaiming in a loud voice his literary maturity, and consequent responsibility, shamelessly prints and publishes such a piece of writing as this sonnet on *Nuptial Sleep*.

[*The essay continues with an examination of individual poems; Buchanan objects to the general fleshliness of all Rossetti's poems, his imitative ability, his rhymes (was/grass, death/hath, love/of, once/suns), and his burdens. Rossetti, he concludes, will be forgotten along with other "once prosperous nonsense-writers each now consigned to his own little limbo." His list of forgotten poets contains Skelton, Gower, Donne, Carew, Cowley, and others.*
Here are his views on " The Blessed Damozel:"]

Amid all his "affluence of jewel-coloured words," he has not given us one rounded and noteworthy piece of art, though his verses are all art; not one poem which is memorable for its own sake, and quite separable from the displeasing identity of the composer. The nearest approach to a perfect whole is the *Blessed Damozel*, a peculiar poem, placed first in the book, perhaps by accident, perhaps because it is a key to the poems which follow. This poem appeared in a rough shape many years ago in the *Germ*, an unwholesome periodical started by the Pre-Raphaelites, and suffered, after gasping through a few feeble numbers, to die the death of all such publications. In spite of its affected title, and of numberless affectations throughout the text, the *Blessed Damozel* has great merits of its own, and a few lines of real genius. We have heard it described as the record of actual grief and love, or, in simple words, the apotheosis of one actually lost by the writer; but, without having any private knowledge of the circumstance of its composition, we feel that such an account of the poem is inadmissible. It does not contain one single note of sorrow. It is a 'composition,' and a clever one. Read the opening stanzas:

> The blessed damozel leaned out
> From the gold bar of Heaven;
> Her eyes were deeper than the depth
> Of waters stilled at even;
> She had three lilies in her hand,
> And the stars in her hair were seven.
>
> Her robe, ungirt from clasp to hem,
> No wrought flowers did adorn,
> But a white rose of Mary's gift,
> For service meetly worn;
> Her hair that lay along her back
> Was yellow like ripe corn.

This is a careful sketch for a picture, which, worked into actual colour by a master, might have been worth seeing. The steadiness of hand lessens as the poem proceeds, and although there are several passages of considerable power—such as that where, far down the void,

> this earth
> Spins like a fretful midge,

or that other, describing how

> the curled moon
> Was like a little feather
> Fluttering far down the gulf.

the general effect is that of a queer old painting in a missal, very affected and very odd. What moved the British critic to ecstasy in this poem seems to us very sad nonsense indeed, or, if not sad nonsense, very meretricious affectation. Thus we have seen the following verses quoted with enthusiasm, as italicised—

> And still she bowed herself and stooped
> Out of the circling charm;
> *Until her bosom must have made*
> *The bar she leaned on warm,*
> And the lilies lay as if asleep
> Along her bended arm.

> From the fixed place of Heaven she saw
> *Time like a pulse shake fierce*
> *Thro' all the worlds.* Her gaze still strove
> Within the gulf to pierce
> Its path; and now she spoke as when
> The stars sang in their spheres.

It seems to us that all these lines are very bad, with the exception of the two admirable lines ending the first verse, and that the italicised portions are quite without merit, and almost without meaning. On the whole, one feels disheartened and amazed at the poet who, in the nineteenth century, talks about "damozels," "citherns," and "citoles," and addresses the mother of Christ as the "Lady Mary"—

> With her five handmaidens, whose names
> Are five sweet symphonies,
> Cecily, Gertrude, Magdalen,
> Margaret and Rosalys.

A suspicion is awakened that the writer is laughing at us. We hover uncertainly between picturesqueness and namby-pamby, and the effect, as Artemus Ward would express it, is "weakening to the intellect." The thing would have been almost too much in the shape of a picture, though the workmanship might have made amends. The truth is that literature, and more particularly poetry, is in a very bad way when one art gets hold of another, and imposes upon it its conditions and limitations. In the first few verses of the *Damozel* we have the subject, or part of the subject, of a picture, and the inventor should either have painted it or left it alone altogether; and, had he done the latter, the world would have lost nothing. Poetry is something more than painting; and an idea will not become a poem because it is too smudgy for a picture.

.   .   .   .

We cannot forbear expressing our wonder, by the way, at the kind of women whom it seems the unhappy lot of these gentlemen to encounter. We have lived as long in the world as they have, but never yet came across persons of the other sex who conduct themselves in the manner described. Females who bite, scratch, scream, bubble, munch, sweat, writhe, twist, wriggle, foam, and in a general way slaver over their lovers, must surely possess some extraordinary qualities to counter-act their otherwise most offensive mode of conducting them-selves. It appears, however, on examination, that their poet-lovers conduct themselves in a similar manner. They, too, bite, scratch, scream, bubble, munch, sweat, writhe, twist, wriggle, foam, and slaver, in a style frightful to hear of. Let us hope that it is only their fun, and that they don't mean half they say.

.   .   .   .

[" *Jenny*" *he dismisses thus:*]

The soliloquy is long, and in some parts beautiful, despite a very constant suspicion that we are listening to an emas-culated Mr Browning, whose whole tone and gesture, so to speak, is occasionally introduced with startling fidelity; and there are here and there glimpses of actual thought and insight over and above the picturesque touches which belong to the writer's true profession, such as that where, at daybreak—

> lights creep in
> Past the gauze curtains half drawn-to
> And *the lamp's doubled shade grows blue.*

What we object to in this poem is not the subject, which any writer may be fairly left to choose for himself; nor anything particularly vicious in the poetic treatment of it; nor any bad blood bursting through in special passages. But the whole tone, without being more than usually coarse, seems heartless. There is not a drop of piteousness in Mr Rossetti. He is just to the outcast, even generous; severe to the seducer; sad even at the spectacle of lust in dimity and fine ribbons. Notwithstanding all this, and a certain delicacy and refinement of treatment unusual with this poet, the poem repels and revolts us, and we like Mr Rossetti least after its perusal. We are angry with the fleshly person at last. The *Blessed Damozel* puzzled us, the *Song of the Bower* amused us, the love sonnet depressed and sickened us, but *Jenny*, tho' distinguished by less special viciousness of thought and style than any of these, fairly makes us lose patience. We detect its fleshliness at a glance; we perceive that the scene was fascinating less through its human tenderness than because it, like all the others, possessed an inherent quality of animalism.

[*Understandably incensed by this article, Rossetti prepared a pamphlet in reply but decided not to risk legal proceedings by publishing it. Instead an abridged version of it appeared under the title "The Stealthy School of Criticism" in "The Athenaeum" of December 16, 1871. The use of the Maitland pseudonym at the end of the "Fleshly School" essay, which had contained several commendatory allusions to his own poetry, had already aroused indignant controversy in the columns of "The Athenaeum." The nineteenth century preferred anonymity in its critical reviews and regarded a pseudonymous signature as dishonest. At the end of Rossetti's essay was a printed letter from Buchanan asserting that his publishers had used the pseudonym without his knowledge or consent, but it was too late. By emphasizing what he called the "Siamese aspect" of Buchanan's identity and by demonstrating that several of Buchanan's quotations of his work had had their meaning deliberately distorted by being removed from their context Rossetti effectively discredited his opponent's article in an essay noteworthy for its restraint and gentle irony. The following passages are taken from the latter part of this essay. From the discussion of "Jenny" with which this extract opens he proceeds to a consideration of wider issues.]*

From "The Stealthy School of Criticism"

Neither some thirteen years ago, when I wrote this poem, nor last year when I published it, did I fail to foresee impending charges of recklessness and aggressiveness, or to perceive that even some among those who could really *read* the poem and acquit me on these grounds, might still hold that the thought in it had better have dispensed with the situation which serves it for framework. Nor did I omit to consider how far a treatment from without might here be possible. But the motive powers of art reverse the requirement of science, and demand first of all an *inner* standing-point. The heart of such a mystery as this must be plucked from the very world in which it beats or bleeds; and the beauty and pity, the self-questionings and all-questionings which it brings with it, can come with full force only from the mouth of one alive to its whole appeal, such as the speaker put forward in the poem—that is, of a young and thoughtful man of the world. To such a speaker, many half-cynical revulsions of feeling and reverie, and a recurrent presence of the impressions of beauty (however artificial) which first brought him within such a circle of influence, would be inevitable features of the dramatic relation portrayed. Here again I can give the lie, in hearing of honest readers, to the base or trivial ideas which my critic labours to connect with the poem. There is another little charge, however, which this minstrel in mufti brings against *Jenny*, namely, one of plagiarism from that very poetic self of his which the tutelary prose does but enshroud for the moment. This question can, fortunately, be settled with ease by others who have read my critic's poems; and thus I need the less regret that, not happening myself to be in that position, I must be content to rank with those who cannot pretend to an opinion on the subject.

It would be humiliating, need one come to serious detail, to have to refute such an accusation as that of "binding oneself by solemn league and covenant to extol fleshliness as the distinct and supreme end of poetic and pictorial art"; and one cannot but feel that here every one will think it allowable merely to pass by with a smile the foolish fellow who has brought a charge thus framed against any reasonable man. Indeed, what I have said already is substantially enough to refute it, even did I not feel sure that a fair balance of my poetry must, of itself, do so in the eyes of every candid reader. I say nothing of my pictures; but those who know them will laugh at the idea. That I may, nevertheless, take a wider view than some poets or critics, of how much, in the material conditions absolutely given to man to deal with as distinct from his spiritual aspirations, is admissible within the limits of Art—this, I say, is possible enough; nor do I wish to shrink from such responsibility. But to state that I do so to the ignoring or overshadowing of spiritual beauty, is an absolute falsehood, impossible to be put forward except in the indulgence of prejudice or rancour.

I have selected, amid much railing on my critic's part, what seemed the most representative indictment against me, and have, so far, answered it. Its remaining clauses set forth how others and myself "aver that poetic expression is greater than poetic thought . . . and sound superior to sense"—an accusation elsewhere, I observe, expressed by saying that we "wish to create form for its own sake." If writers of verse are to be listened to in such arraignment of each other, it might be quite competent to me to prove, from the works of my friends in question, that no such thing is the case with them; but my present function is to confine myself to my own defence. This again, it is difficult to do quite seriously. It is no part of my undertaking to dispute the verdict of any 'contemporary,' however contemptuous or contemptible, on my own measure of executive success; but the accusation cited above is not against the poetic value of certain work, but against its primary and (by assumption) its admitted aim. And to this I must reply that so far, assuredly, not even Shakespeare himself could desire more arduous human tragedy for development in Art than belongs to the themes I venture to embody, however incalculably higher might be his power of dealing with them. What more inspiring for poetic effort than the terrible Love turned to Hate—perhaps the deadliest of all passion-woven complexities—which is the theme of *Sister Helen*, and, in a more fantastic form, of *Eden Bower*—the surroundings of both poems being the mere machinery of a central universal meaning? What, again, more so than . . . the baffling problems which the face of *Jenny* conjures up—or than the analysis of passion and feeling attempted in *The House of Life*, and others among the more purely lyrical poems? I speak here, as does my critic in the clause adduced, of *aim* not of *achievement*; and so far, the mere summary is instantly subversive of the preposterous imputation. To assert that the poet whose matter is such as this aims chiefly at "creating form for its own sake," is, in fact, almost an ingenuous kind of dishonesty; for surely it delivers up the assertor at once, bound hand and foot, to the tender mercies of contradictory proof. Yet this may fairly be taken as an example of the spirit in which a constant effort is here made against me to appeal to those who either are ignorant of what I write, or else belong to the large class too easily influenced by an assumption of authority in addressing them. The false name appended to the article must, as is evident, aid this position vastly; for who, after all, would not be apt to laugh at seeing one poet confessedly come forward as aggressor against another in the field of criticism?

It would not be worth while to lose time and patience in noticing minutely how the system of misrepresentation is carried into points of artistic detail—giving us, for example, such statements as that the burthen employed in the ballad of *Sister Helen* "is repeated with little or no alteration through thirty-four verses," whereas the fact is, that the alteration of it in every verse is the very scheme of the poem. But these are minor matters quite thrown into the shade by the critic's more daring sallies. In addition to the class of attack I have answered above, the article contains, of course, an immense amount of personal paltriness; as, for instance, attributions of my work to this, that, or the other absurd derivative source; or again, pure nonsense (which can have no real meaning even to the writer) about "one art getting hold of another, and imposing on it its conditions and limitations"; or, indeed, what not besides? However, to such antics as this, no more attention is possible than that which Virgil enjoined Dante to bestow on the meaner phenomena of his pilgrimage.

[*Undeterred, Buchanan returned to the attack in 1872, publishing "The Fleshly School of Poetry and other Phenomena of the Day." This comprised a contemptuous dismissal of Rossetti's defence; a version of the earlier essay modified in places and with its quotations more accurately produced, but substantially the same as before; and a good deal of fresh matter which attempts to indicate the rapid growth of sensuality in all contemporary writing. This he attributes to the continental influence, especially Baudelaire; he enlarges the scope of his attack to include Swinburne as well as Rossetti in a chapter called "Pearls from the Amatory Poets" where passages of their poems and of the Metaphysicals (including Donne) are held up to ridicule. This time it was Swinburne who replied and virtually ended the controversy by his scathing "Under the Microscope" (1872). In the 1880's Buchanan changed his attitude to Rossetti before the latter's death and later wrote to Hall Caine:*

I make full admission of Rossetti's claims to the purest kind of literary renown; and, if I were to criticize his poems now, I would write very differently.]

WALTER PATER

DANTE GABRIEL ROSSETTI

[*Steeped as he was in European literature and art, an authority on the Italian Renaissance and a man of wide culture, Pater was better equipped than Buchanan for a sympathetic approach to the poetry of Rossetti. The following is an abridgement of an essay written in 1883 in which Pater evaluates Rossetti's aims and achievement.*

After praising Rossetti's sincerity and the originality of his "wholly natural expression of certain wonderful things he really felt and saw," Pater continues:]

One of the peculiarities of *The Blessed Damozel* was a definiteness of sensible imagery, which seemed almost grotesque to some, and was strange, above all, in a theme so profoundly visionary. The gold bar of heaven from which she leaned, her hair yellow like ripe corn, are but examples of a general treatment, as naively detailed as the pictures of those early painters contemporary with Dante, who has shown a similar care for minute and definite imagery in his verse; there, too, in the very midst of profoundly mystic vision. Such definition of outline is indeed one among many points in which Rossetti resembles the great Italian poet, of whom, led to him at first by family circumstances, he was ever a lover—a "servant and singer," faithful as Dante, "of Florence and of Beatrice"—with some close inward conformities of genius also, independent of any mere circumstances of education. It was said by a critic of the last century, not wisely though agreeably to the practice of his time, that poetry rejoices in abstractions. For Rossetti, as for Dante, without question on his part, the first condition of the poetic way of seeing and presenting things is particularisation.

And this delight in concrete definition is allied with another of his conformities to Dante, the really imaginative vividness, namely, of his personifications—his hold upon them, or rather their hold upon him, with the force of a Frankenstein, when once they have taken life from him. Not Death only and Sleep, for instance, and the winged spirit of Love, but certain particular aspects of them, a whole "populace" of special hours and places, "the hour" even "which might have been, yet might not be," are living creatures, with hands and eyes and articulate voices. . . .

With him indeed, as in some revival of the old mythopoeic age, common things—dawn, noon, night—are full of human or personal expression, full of sentiment. The lovely little sceneries scattered up and down his poems, glimpses of a landscape, not indeed of broad open-air effects, but rather that of a painter concentrated upon the picturesque effect of one or two selected objects at a time—the "hollow brimmed with mist," or the "ruined weir," as he sees it from one of his windows, or reflected in one of the mirrors of his "house of life" (the vignettes for instance seen by Rose Mary in the magic beryl) attest, by their very freshness and simplicity, to a pictorial or descriptive power in dealing with the inanimate world, which is certainly also one half of the charm, in that other, more remote and mystic, use of it. For with Rossetti this sense of lifeless nature, after all, is translated to a higher service, in which it does but incorporate itself with some phase of strong emotion. Every one understands how this may happen at critical moments of life; . . . To Rossetti it is so always, because to him life is a crisis at every moment. A sustained impressibility towards the mysterious conditions of man's everyday life, towards the very mystery itself in it, gives a singular gravity to all his work; those matters never became trite to him. But throughout, it is the ideal intensity of love—of love based upon a perfect yet peculiar type of physical or material beauty—which is enthroned in the midst of those mysterious powers; Youth and Death, Destiny and Fortune, Fame, Poetic Fame, Memory, Oblivion, and the like. Rossetti is one of those who, in the words of Merimée, *se passionnent pour la passion*, one of Love's lovers.

And yet, again as with Dante, to speak of his ideal type of beauty as material, is partly misleading. Spirit and matter, indeed, have been for the most part opposed, with a false contrast or antagonism by schoolmen, whose artificial creation those abstractions really are. In our actual concrete experience the two trains of phenomena which the words *matter* and *spirit* do but roughly distinguish, play inextricably into each other. Practically, the church of the Middle Age by its æsthetic worship, its sacramentalism, its real faith in the resurrection of the flesh, had set itself against that Manichean opposition of spirit and matter, and its results in men's way of taking life; and in this Dante is the central representative of its spirit. To him, in the vehement and impassioned heat of his conceptions, the material and the spiritual are fused and blent: if the spiritual attains the definite visibility of a crystal, what is material loses its earthiness and impurity. And here again, by force of instinct, Rossetti is one with him. His chosen type of beauty is one,

> Whose speech Truth knows not from her thought,
> Nor Love her body from her soul.

Like Dante, he knows no region of spirit which shall not be sensuous also, or material. The shadowy world, which he realises so powerfully, has still the ways and houses, the land and water, the light and darkness, the fire and flowers, that had so much to do in the moulding of those bodily powers and aspects which counted for so large a part of the soul, here. . . .

Notwithstanding this, his work, it must be conceded, certainly through no narrowness or egotism, but in the faithfulness of a true workman to a vocation so emphatic, was mainly of the esoteric order. But poetry, at all times, exercises two distinct functions: it may reveal, it may unveil to every eye, the ideal aspects of common things, after Gray's way (though Gray too, it is well to remember, seemed in his own day, seemed even to Johnson, obscure) or it may actually add to the number of motives poetic and uncommon in themselves, by the imaginative creation of things that are ideal from their very birth. Rossetti did something, something excellent, of the former kind; but his characteristic, his really revealing work, lay in the adding to poetry of fresh poetic material, of a new order of phenomena, in the creation of a new ideal.

NOTES

INTRODUCTION

p. 13. *Robert Buchanan*. See pp. 176–184, and pp. 207–208.

p. 13. *Oscar Wilde's opinion*. See *The Critic as Artist*, Part I.

p. 13. *Ruskin. . . classifies painters*. See *Modern Painters* iv, chapter vii, section 18.

p. 15. *an amateur who failed*. Ford Madox Hueffer in *Rossetti* (London, 1902) quotes this at p. 83, but does not cite the originator of the comment.

p. 16. *the favourite source . . . was Shakespeare*. A complete enumeration of all Pre-Raphaelite Shakespeare illustrations is impossible. Rossetti did drawings or paintings of scenes from *Hamlet, Macbeth, Othello, and Measure for Measure*; Holman Hunt did an oil painting of *Claudio and Isabella*, while Madox Brown made sixteen pen-and-ink drawings and three oils of scenes from *King Lear* as well as one oil *Romeo and Juliet*. W. M. Rossetti records "that the very first book my brother took to with strong personal zest" was an illustrated *Hamlet* which he acquired at the age of four or five (*Dante Gabriel Rossetti: Letters and Memoir* (London, 1895), vol. i, p. 58).

p. 17. *The famous Moxon edition*. Illustrations from this will be found at pp. 17, 35, 68, and 72. It included in all eighteen drawings by Millais, seven by Hunt, and five by Rossetti. See also notes at pp. 210, 211. Moxon also published an edition of Byron, for which Madox Brown made several designs.

p. 17. *Writing to Allingham*. See *Letters of D. G. Rossetti to William Allingham, 1854–70*, edited by G. Birkbeck Hill (London, 1897), p. 97.

p. 19. *"The Germ."* This periodical survived for only four numbers (January, February, March, and May 1850), changing its title in No. 3. It was edited by W. M. Rossetti, who wrote an introductory pamphlet to a facsimile reprint of the four numbers published in 1901, in which he reproduces contemporary press notices of the magazine, including that from *The Critic* quoted at p. 20, and annotates pseudonyms used by the various contributors. Versions of the following items included in the present volume appeared in *The Germ*: by D. G. Rossetti, *Hand and Soul*, *My Sister's Sleep*, *The Blessed Damozel*; by W. M. Rossetti, a sonnet; by F. G. Stephens, *The Purpose and Tendency of Early Italian Art*; by Thomas Woolner, *My Beautiful Lady*. In addition to these and other works by the same authors *The Germ* contained *inter alia* several poems by Christina Rossetti under the pseudonym of "Ellen Alleyn," poems and an essay on *Macbeth* by Coventry Patmore (anonymously), and etchings by Holman Hunt (see p. 128), Collinson, Madox Brown, and Deverell.

p. 20. *W. M. Rossetti . . . records*. *Pre-Raphaelite Diaries and Letters* (London, 1900), p. 228. In his *D. G. Rossetti: Letters and Memoir* (vol. i, p. 421) he quotes a letter from his brother to Hall Caine admitting "that my friends here consider me exceptionally averse to politics; and I suppose I must be, for I never read a Parliamentary Debate in my life."

p. 23. *Brown's commentary* [on *Work*]. Reproduced at pp. 51–58.

p. 23. *the Everlasting Yea of Sartor Resartus*. See Book II, chapter 9. The concluding lines of this passage may be compared with Rossetti's *Hand and Soul* at p. 77.

p. 24. *Morris in a pamphlet*. *The Aims of Art*, reprinted in *Signs of Change*, 1888. See extract at pp. 59–65.

p. 25. *Even his grandson . . . complains*. F. M. Hueffer: *Ford Madox Brown* (London, 1896), p. 414.

p. 25. *All art from the beginning*. Hunt, *op. cit.*, vol. ii, chapter xvi, p. 463.

p. 25. *"The Awakened Conscience."* Hunt's comments on this will be found in his *op. cit.*, vol. ii, chapter xv, pp. 429–430. I have retained the form of the title which Hunt uses *passim*, but Ruskin and others regularly call it *The Awakening Conscience*. These passages are reproduced by kind permission of Mrs Michael Joseph.

p. 26. *Ruskin exclaimed with enthusiasm*. In a letter to *The Times*, May 25, 1854; see Library Edition of Ruskin, vol. xii, p. 334. The passage quoted at pp. 36–37 is from the same letter.

p. 30. *Hunt devotes a good deal of time*. See Hunt, *op. cit.*, vol. ii, chapter xv, pp. 427–433.

p. 30. *Scott in his "Autobiographical Notes."* *Autobiographical Notes of the Life of William Bell Scott* (edited by W. Minto; London, 1892), vol. i, pp. 289 and 293.

p. 31. *"The Unclassed."* See chapter xxvi.

p. 34. *"The Blind Girl" which Rossetti described*. See *The Letters of Dante Gabriel Rossetti to William Allingham, 1854–70*, p. 181.

p. 34.   "*The Carpenter's Shop.*"   An alternative title for Millais' *Christ in the House of His Parents*.   See Dickens's commentary on that picture at p. 174 of the present volume where the title was first used derogatorily.

p. 34.   *Bell Scott records Millais.*   See Scott, *op. cit.*, vol. i, p. 278.

p. 35.   *as Scott suggests.*   Scott, *op. cit.*, vol. i, p. 251:

> the seed of the flower of Pre-Raphaelism [*sic*] was photography. The seriousness and honesty of motive, the unerring fatalism of the sun's action, as well as the perfection of the impression on the eye, was what it aspired to. . . .   The execution was to be like the binocular representations of leaves that the stereoscope was then beginning to show.

An Arts Council Festival of Britain exhibition of Masterpieces of Victorian Photography held at the Victoria and Albert Museum in 1951 afforded an interesting opportunity of comparing Pre-Raphaelite art with contemporary photography.   The photographs came from the Helmut Gernsheim collection, and these, together with Mr Gernsheim's catalogue to the exhibition, make the following note possible.

Between 1843 and 1848 two Scotsmen, D. O. Hill and R. Adamson, were making photographic history with pictures such as *Miss Chalmers and Her Brother* (1843) and *The Rev. James Fairbairn reading to Fishwives at Newhaven near Edinburgh* (*c.* 1845), the arrangement, anecdotal nature, and atmosphere of which have a marked Pre-Raphaelite flavour, as has W. H. Fox Talbot's *The Open Door* (1844).   There is no evidence of the P.R.B. being familiar with these works, though in later years all of them took a lively interest in the new art of photography.   Hill was himself a painter, and these photographs are carefully arranged pictorial compositions.   Clearly the two arts were seen in very close relation, and these photographic studies made to look like paintings may well have influenced painters.   In the 1850's Roger Fenton's photography reached such a standard of realism that he was accused of plagiarizing the painter George Lance, and many later photographs are clear imitations of the Pre-Raphaelite manner.   One such was Henry Peach Robinson's *The Lady of Shalott* (1861), about which he wrote in 1892:

> I made a barge, crimped the model's long hair, P.R. fashion, laid her on the boat in the river among the water lilies, and gave her a background of weeping willows, taken in the rain that they might look dreary; and really they were very expressive. . . .   I think I succeeded in making the picture very Pre-Raphaelite, very weird,

and very untrue to nature—I mean imaginative; but it was a ghastly mistake to attempt such a subject in our realistic art.

However current this use of the term may have become by 1892, the original brotherhood would have been very shocked to find 'Pre-Raphaelite' used as synonymous with "very weird, and very untrue to nature."

p. 36. *Ruskin, defending " The Awakened Conscience."* See note to p. 26 above.

p. 38. *murals for the Oxford Union.* As the painters did not realize the need to prepare the wall surface specially, but painted direct on whitewash, the murals perished; they were restored in 1936 by Professor Tristram.

p. 39. *one modern critic.* R. H. Wilenski, *An Outline of English Painting* (London, 1946), p. 66: "As in *King Cophetua and the Beggar Maid* (Tate Gallery) he only achieved crudely coloured still-life records of models posing in Wardour Street surroundings."

p. 42. *his own dictum.* In *The Beauty of Life* (1880).

p. 42. *Sir Thomas Bodkin.* See *The Approach to Painting* (London, 1927, revised 1945), pp. 66 and 69. Sir Thomas is referring to Frith initially, but his remarks are extended to include the Pre-Raphaelites and others.

p. 43. *W. B. Yeats.* See in this connexion Graham Hough, *The Last Romantics* (London, 1949).

p. 43. *Bernard Shaw.* The quotations are from the Preface to the Penguin edition of *Pygmalion* and the Preface to *Plays Pleasant* respectively.

p. 43. *D. H. Lawrence.* See *The Letters of D. H. Lawrence*, edited by A. Huxley (London, 1932), p. 3; *Selected Essays* (London, 1950), p. 318; and Anthony West, *D. H. Lawrence* (London, 1950), chapter ix.

p. 43. *Isaac Rosenberg.* See "The Pre-Raphaelites and Imagination in Paint," an essay included in *The Collected Poems of Isaac Rosenberg*, edited by Gordon Bottomley and D. W. Harding (Chatto and Windus, 1937), p. 257. Reprinted here by kind permission of the publishers and the author's sister, Mrs Wynick.

PRE-RAPHAELITE WRITINGS ON ART

The passages in this section have been chosen as illustrating, by their diversity of viewpoint, something of the complexity of Pre-

Raphaelitism. F. G. Stephens's essay explains what the original P.R.B. found admirable in Italian art before Raphael, and urges the moral significance of art with more fire than Hunt in his retrospective survey; similarly W. M. Rossetti's plea for sincerity in the artist and tolerance in the audience is as much the work of a young man as is Bell Scott's parallel sonnet, while Hunt's anxiety to do justice to Sir Joshua Reynolds and Raphael clearly does not belong to the period when the young P.R.B. was grounding its artistic faith in a bold antipathy to both. Ford Madox Brown's commentary on his own *Work*, besides being an example of literature as an accessory to painting, shows Pre-Raphaelitism commenting on the society of its own day, but it tacitly accepts the *status quo* in a way that William Morris certainly does not in his thorough-going attack on Philistinical capitalism as an obstacle to art, an attack which orginates in something akin to the medievalism which Holman Hunt distrusts and yet is closer to actuality than Hunt's narrow and prejudiced moral fervour. Morris's concept of the pleasure-giving, recreative aim of art is also in direct contrast to Stephens's insistence on its didactic function. Hunt's summary of the Brotherhood's aims from the detachment of old age does not, with the insularity and inconsistencies of its argument, maintain the objectivity it attempts, but it is of interest for its concern with the literary antecedents of the movement and for its qualified reassertion, after sixty years, of what Hunt conceived to be the principles of that movement.

p. 45, **F. G. Stephens**
  b. London 1828. Accidentally lamed for life as a child. Studied with Hunt at the R.A. Schools, and nominated by him for membership of the original P.R.B. Exhibited at the Academy 1852 and 1854, but later turned to criticism instead of creative work, becoming Art Critic of *The Athenæum* 1861–1901 and publishing many books on art including *Dante Gabriel Rossetti* (London, 1894). Died Hammersmith 1907.

p. 45. THE PURPOSE AND TENDENCY OF EARLY ITALIAN ART. This appeared in *The Germ*, No. 2, February 1850, pp. 58–64, and is reproduced by courtesy of James A. Iggulden, Esq. Stephens used the pseudonym "John Seward" for this essay. He contributed to *The Germ*, No. 4, as "Laura Savage."

p. 46. *the modern artist does not retire to monasteries.* The closeness of association between Pre-Raphaelite art and religion is emphasized by the fact that one member of the P.R.B., James Collinson

(1825–81), becoming a convert to Roman Catholicism, did spend about four years as a Jesuit novice in Stonyhurst from 1851. His engagement to Christina Rossetti was broken off because of his Catholicism, she being an Anglican.

p. 46. *to represent the thing and the whole of the thing.* That this view of the function of art was a feature of the age may be shown by Arnold's insistence on knowledge "to see the object as in itself it really is," and his praise of those "who saw Life steadily, and saw it whole."

p. 47. *Niello work.* A form of decorative work particularly delicate and minute, much practised in Florence in the fifteenth century; it consists in filling with a black metallic amalgam lines incised on a polished metal surface.

p. 48. *Gozzoli* (1424–97). A Florentine painter, pupil of Fra Angelico. An account of his work will be found in Crowe and Cavalcaselle: *History of Painting in Italy* (London, 1903–14), vol. iv, chapter xv. This work does not record a 'Vineyard' of his, but Stephens is probably referring to his fresco *Noah's Drunkenness* (in the Camposanto, Pisa; reproduced *op. cit.*, p. 358), where the left-hand half of the scene is a vineyard as described. See W. M. Rossetti: *D. G. Rossetti: Letters and Memoir*, vol. i, p. 125.

p. 48. *Ghiberti* (1378–1455). Famous for his great bronze doors to the Baptistery at Florence, at which he worked from 1403 until his death. One door has carvings of twenty scenes from the life of Christ, the four Evangelists and the four Doctors of the Church; the other has ten Old Testament scenes. These have been admirably reproduced in *Ghiberti*, by Ludwig Goldscheider (London, 1949). There was a cast of these doors at the Academy Schools, which Hunt and Rossetti admired and copied. (See W. M. Rossetti, *Memoir*, vol. i, pp. 96–97).

p. 48. The other painters to whom Stephens refers in this paragraph are Florentine fresco painters of the Middle Ages. The P.R.B. had access to their work in a volume of what Ruskin called "Lasinio's execrable engravings" which they found at Millais' home in 1848, and both Hunt and W. M. Rossetti agree on the importance of the influence of these on the formation of the Brotherhood. References against their names are to relevant chapters in Crowe and Cavalcaselle, *op. cit.* Fra Angelico (Stephens spelt it 'Angilico'), 1387–1455 (vol. iv, chapter iv), Masaccio, 1401–*c.* 1428 (vol. iv, chapter iii), Ghirlandaio, 1449–94 (vol. iv, chapter xiv); Orcagna, 1308–68 (vol. ii, chapter xiii); and Giotto, *c.* 1267–1337 (vol. ii, chapters ii, iii, and v). Baccio della Porta, known also as Fra Bartolommeo, 1475–1517.

p. 51, **William Michael Rossetti**
b. 1829, brother of Dante Gabriel Rossetti. Made secretary of P.R.B., edited *The Germ* and contributed poetry and poetry reviews to it. Later became self-appointed historian to the movement. Edited the works of Blake, Byron, Shelley, D. G. Rossetti, Christina Rossetti, *et alia.* Publications include: *Dante Gabriel Rossetti: his Family Letters, with a Memoir* (London, 1895, two vols.), *Ruskin: Rossetti: Pre-Raphaelitism* (London, 1899), *Pre-Raphaelite Diaries and Letters* (London, 1900), *Rossetti Papers, 1862–70* (London, 1903), and the Preface to the 1901 facsimile reprint of *The Germ.* By profession a civil servant, he became art critic of *The Critic* in summer of 1850 and of *The Spectator* later in the same year. Died 1919.

This sonnet appeared on the cover of each issue of *The Germ* and *Art and Poetry*; of it Bell Scott says (*Autobiographical Notes*, vol. i, p. 324):

> When one has mastered this production, though indeed it would almost need a Browning Society's united intellects, it will be found to mean that the only desirable and vital workmanship is that which honestly and directly expresses our own conceptions and observations; and this is the one excellence we find in all the works of the brethren.

This and the passage at p. 20 are reproduced by kind permission of Mrs Imogen Dennis.

p. 51, **Ford Madox Brown**
b. Calais 1821. Studied art on the Continent, where he met and came under the influence of the German 'Nazarene' or 'Pre-Raphaelite' painters, Cornelius and Overbeck. Returned to England 1846. D. G. Rossetti became his pupil for a short time in 1848, and although Brown was never formally a member of the P.R.B. his work reflects all its principles most faithfully. Literariness of theme is represented in his *Wickliffe reading the Bible to John of Gaunt* and *Chaucer in the House of Edward III* as well as in the illustrations and paintings referred to in the Introduction. He contributed poetry, an essay, and an etching to *The Germ*, and also wrote a number of sonnets for pictures, the literary merit of which is slight; indeed, this prose passage shows him as a forceful rather than an elegant and coherent writer. Best known for his *Work* and *The Last of England* (a portrait of

himself and his wife inspired by the emigration of Thomas Woolner (*q.v.*) to Australia in 1852), he is also a good landscape painter and between 1878 and 1893 was commissioned to paint frescoes in Manchester Town Hall. Died London 1893.

Work is reproduced at p. 97. His diary is published in W. M. Rossetti's *Pre-Raphaelite Diaries and Letters*, and there is a full-length biography and critical study by his grandson: *Ford Madox Brown*, by Ford M. Hueffer (Longmans, Green and Co., 1896). This commentary is taken from that volume (pp. 189–195) and is reproduced by courtesy of the publishers. Hueffer does not state its exact origin or purpose. Picture and commentary are considered at pp. 22–25 of the Introduction to the present volume. The picture was completed in 1863.

p. 56. *The Boys' Home, 41 Euston Road.* An actual institution in which Brown took a charitable interest.

p. 57. *Professor Snoöx.* "One of the imaginary companions of D. G. Rossetti. With his fellow Ornithorhyncus Bug (Snoöx's Christian name being Athanasius) he made about this time—or, perhaps, before the death of Mrs D. G. Rossetti—constant appearances in the conversation of the poet-artist's more wayward moods." (Hueffer, *op. cit.*, p. 196.)

p. 57. *The episode of the policeman.* Not easily distinguished in small-scale reproductions, this incident will be found on the extreme right of the picture, behind the two "brain-workers."

p. 58. *personages of note.* Hueffer records that these were Thomas Carlyle (the "brain-worker" with a hat), Frederick Denison Maurice (his companion), and R. B. Martineau the artist as the man on the horse (a fact which gives added point to Brown's comment on him at p. 56). Brown's wife was the model for the beautiful young rich lady, and his infant son Arthur, who died in 1857, was the baby.

p, 59, **William Morris**
b. Walthamstow 1834. Educated at Marlborough and Exeter College, Oxford, where he met Burne-Jones (*q.v.*). Contributed stories and poems to *The Oxford and Cambridge Magazine* 1856. At Rossetti's instigation gave up his intended architectural career for painting, and in 1857 collaborated with Rossetti on the frescoes for the Oxford Union. Published *The Defence of Guenevere and Other Poems* (1858). Married, 1859, Jane Burden, the model of the drawing by Rossetti at p. 144. In 1861 founded firm of Morris, Marshall, Faulkner and Co., interior decorators and

makers of furniture and furnishings, many of which Morris designed; and in 1890–91 founded the Kelmscott Press.

Verse publications include *The Life and Death of Jason* (1867), *The Earthly Paradise* (1868–70), and *Sigurd the Volsung* (1877). He translated the *Æneid*, the *Odyssey*, *Beowulf*, and some Icelandic sagas, and published a series of long prose romances in the last ten years of his life. Taking an active interest in politics and education, he began lecturing on the arts in 1877 and on the social problems that he regarded as inseparable from the arts, and wrote many prose pamphlets; this passage is taken from one such lecture and contains ample evidence of being written for the speaking voice. He also published *Chants for Socialists* (1884–85) and *The Pilgrims of Hope* (1886), two volumes of political poetry, and helped to found the Socialist League. *A Dream of John Ball* (1888) was a medieval prose romance with a topical political application, and his Utopian *News from Nowhere* (1890) represents the fusion of his Pre-Raphaelite ideals of art and craftsmanship with his political beliefs. Died Hammersmith 1896.

The standard biography is J. W. Mackail's of 1899. A good selection of his writings is available, edited G. D. H. Cole (London, 1946), and his artistic achievement is well represented in *William Morris, Designer*, by Gerald H. Crow (London, 1934). The passage quoted here is from *The Aims of Art*, published as a pamphlet in 1887, republished in *Signs of Change* (1888). It illustrates how his belief in Socialism developed from his love of medievalism, and should be read in conjunction with his *Gothic Architecture* (1889), and the other pamphlets and lectures in *Hopes and Fears for Art* (1882) and *Signs of Change*, and *Art and Socialism* (1884). Other work by Morris will be found at pp. 129–165. His old home, the Water House, Walthamstow, is now a museum containing a wide selection of his work.

p. 60. *a pleasure which no one can ever have again.* Later in this essay Morris explains:

> Neither phalanstere nor dynamite has swept its beauty away, its destroyers have not been either the philanthropist or the Socialist, the co-operator or the anarchist. It has been sold, and at a cheap price indeed: muddled away by the greed and incompetence of fools who do not know what life and pleasure mean . . . and whose name is Commercial Profit.

p. 65, **William Holman Hunt, O.M., D.C.L.**
  b. 1827. Student from 1844 in the R.A. Schools where he met

Millais and Rossetti (*q.v.*), with whom he founded the Pre-Raphaelite Brotherhood in 1848. Visited Palestine 1854, 1869, and 1873, in order to paint scenes from the life of Christ with the maximum accuracy; his two best-known pictures of the Holy Land are *The Scapegoat* and *The Finding of Christ in the Temple*. The second, completed on his return to England, the model for Christ being found in London, was sold to the dealer Gambart for 5500 guineas, the highest price ever paid up to that date for a contemporary picture in this country. Other works of Hunt's are reproduced at pp. 68, 72, 96, and 128 of this volume and discussed in the Introduction. Alone, perhaps, of the P.R.B., he knew exactly what he meant by Pre-Raphaelitism and continued to paint in that style throughout his life. His monumental *Pre-Raphaelitism and the Pre-Raphaelite Brotherhood* (Macmillan, 1905, 1906, two vols.), from which these extracts are taken, is idiosyncratic to a point with which Rossetti and Morris would probably have disagreed strongly, but it is an honest presentation of a point of view and an interesting account of the movement and of Hunt's own life. He was awarded the O.M. in 1905, and died in 1910, being buried in St. Paul's, where there still hangs a replica of his most popular picture, *The Light of the World* (the original is at Keble College, Oxford). The present extracts will be found at *op. cit*, vol. ii, pp. 465–466, 484–485–486, 488–489, and 490–493, and are reproduced by kind permission of Mrs Michael Joseph.

p. 71. *the Caracci and Le Brun*. Caracci: a family of Bolognese painters (*c*. 1600), who taught that art should be based on work of Raphael, Michaelangelo, and Titian. Le Brun (1619–90): French historical painter and 'art dictator' under Louis XIV.

p. 72, William Bell Scott

b. Edinburgh 1811. Though a friend of Rossetti, Scott was employed from 1844 to 1864 in the Government School of Design at Newcastle and was thus not directly connected with the P.R.B. He contributed a poem, *Morning Sleep*, to No. 2 of *The Germ* and a sonnet, *Early Aspirations*, to No. 3. Between 1864 and 1882 he lived near Rossetti in Chelsea and formed a friendship with him which is recorded in *Autobiographical Notes of the Life of William Bell Scott*, edited by W. Minto (London, 1892). His father was an engraver, and his elder brother David Scott (1806–49) the romantic painter. Bell Scott himself illustrated his own poems (see reproduction at p. 123) which appeared in two main volumes: *Poems by William Bell Scott* (London, 1875) and *A*

Poet's Harvest Home (London, 1893.) This poem will be found at p. 183 of the former. He died at Penkill, Ayrshire, in 1890. He seems to have been somewhat querulous in disposition, and he and W. M. Rossetti frequently disagree in their recollection of events. Other poems are at pp. 123–126.

PRE-RAPHAELITE CREATIVE WRITING

p. 74, Dante Gabriel Rossetti

b. London 1828, son of an Italian political refugee. Studied art at the R.A. Schools 1846–48, and as a pupil of Ford Madox Brown 1848. With Hunt and Millais founded the P.R.B. 1848. Examples of his paintings are at pp. 112, 144 and of his drawings at pp. 113, 116, 144, 160. Notes on these are at pp. 211–212.

In 1857 undertook the decoration of the Oxford Union with Burne Jones, Morris, and others (see note at p. 195). In 1860 married Elizabeth Siddal, his model, whose tragic death in 1862 aggravated his melancholic disposition (see p. 213). Although writing poetry since 1847 or earlier, had only published in magazines prior to 1860. Buried a volume of manuscript poems in his wife's coffin, and was persuaded in 1869 to have it exhumed in order to prepare his poems for publication. This action and the circumstances of his wife's death led to notoriety accentuated by the controversy over his poetry (see pp. 176–191). His later life overshadowed by melancholia and drug-taking. Died Birchington, Kent, 1882.

Published *The Early Italian Poets*, translations (London, 1861; revised 1874 and republished as *Dante and his Circle*); *Poems* (London, 1870); *Ballads and Sonnets* (London, 1881). Various collected editions posthumously, edited by W. M. Rossetti.

Biography and criticism: see p. 198 above, under "W. M. Rossetti." Other contemporary works include Sir T. H. Hall Caine, *Recollections of Dante Gabriel Rossetti* (1882), F. G. Stephens (*q.v.*), *Dante Gabriel Rossetti* (1894), A. C. Benson, *Rossetti* (English Men of Letters Series, 1904). More recent studies include Helen Rossetti Angeli (daughter of W. M. Rossetti), *Dante Gabriel Rossetti* (London, 1949); Oswald Doughty, *Dante Gabriel Rossetti: a Victorian Romantic* (Yale, 1949); and R. Waller, *The Rossetti Family, 1824–54* (Manchester, 1932).

The standard work on his art is H. C. Marillier, *Dante Gabriel Rossetti: an Illustrated Memorial of his Art and Life* (London, 1899), of which an abridged version was published in 1904 under the title *Dante Gabriel Rossetti* in the "British Painters" series.

p. 74. HAND AND SOUL. This prose study, which in conception and method anticipates Walter Pater's *Imaginary Portraits*, appeared in the first number of *The Germ*. Not only is it of interest as one of the few published pieces of Rossetti's prose (apart from letters), but it illustrates the fusion between pictorial art, sensuous experience, religion, and mysticism underlying so much of his work, while theme and style suggest the extent of his influence on William Morris. W. M. Rossetti comments (*Memoir*, vol. i, pp. 154–155) that this "shows that Rossetti's knowledge of art-history was at this period extremely slight . . . as it is totally impossible that, at so remote a date as 1239, any painter whatever should have produced a work at all corresponding with the details given concerning this picture." In the Preface to the facsimile of *The Germ* (pp. 18–20) he adds that San Rocco is an anachronism, and in both places he records people taking for fact the imaginary details of art-history with which Rossetti documented this story, and mentions an etching for it made—and subsequently destroyed—by his brother.

p. 79. *Manus Animam pinxit*. "The hand painted the soul."

p. 79. *Schizzo d'autore incerto*. "Sketch by an unknown artist."

p. 80. *Che so? etc*. Translated, this passage reads: "How do I know? Mystic stuff. These English are mad about mysticism—it's like those fogs they have over there. It makes them think of their country:

> and melts their heart in sighs
> The day they have said farewell to their sweet friends."

His companion rejoins, "The night, you mean."

The quotation is from the opening lines of Canto VIII of Dante's *Purgatorio*, and is quoted from Laurence Binyon's translation.

p. 80. *Et toi donc, etc*. The French conversation runs: "And you, what do you think of this kind of painting?" "Me? I, my dear fellow, say that it's a speciality with which I cannot be bothered. I hold that when one can't understand a thing it's therefore of no importance."

p. 81. THE BLESSED DAMOZEL. W. M. Rossetti (*Memoir*, vol. i, p. 107) says this was written in 1847, and continues:

> In 1881 Rossetti gave Mr Caine an account of its origin, as deriving from his perusal and admiration of Edgar Poe's *Raven*. "I saw"

(this is Mr Caine's version of Rossetti's statement) "that Poe had done the utmost it was possible to do with the grief of the lover on earth, and I determined to reverse the conditions, and give utterance to the yearning of the loved one in Heaven." Along with *The Raven*, other poems by Poe—*Ulalume*, *For Annie*, *The Haunted Palace*, and many another—were a deep well of delight to Rossetti in all those years.

The influence of Poe on Pre-Raphaelitism needs fuller investigation than it has yet received. This poem appeared first in the second number of *The Germ* in a longer and verbally different form. Marillier lists six studies for or versions of a pictorial treatment of it (one is at p. 144 of the present volume). Two of these, in oils, have a predella showing the lover on earth gazing heavenward (reproduced by Marillier opposite p. 188). The comments of Buchanan, reprinted at pp. 179–182 of the present volume, should also be noted.

p. 86. MY SISTER'S SLEEP. "Even earlier than *The Blessed Damozel*" (W. M. Rossetti, *Memoir*, vol. i, p. 107). At p. 18 of the Preface to *The Germ* facsimile he remarks: "it is not founded upon any actual event affecting the Rossetti family," and adds that its metre "was not much in use until it became famous in Tennyson's *In Memoriam* published in 1850, and of course totally unknown to Rossetti when he wrote *My Sister's Sleep*." A slightly longer version of this poem also appeared in the first number of *The Germ*.

p. 88. SISTER HELEN. This, "which may have been written in 1851 or early 1852, was first printed in a magazine—German, with an English issue"—in about 1854 (W. M. Rossetti, *Memoir*, vol. i, pp. 166–167).

p. 98. A LAST CONFESSION. Also assigned by W. M. Rossetti to the late 1840's, this is a long dramatic monologue telling a story of passion and violence against a Lombardy background, and contains an Italian lyric and translation, both by Rossetti. See Introduction, p. 33.

p. 99. THE HOUSE OF LIFE. In *Poems* of 1870 this title was given to fifty sonnets and a group of lyrics; in *Ballads and Sonnets* (1881) the lyrics were omitted and the number of sonnets increased to 101. The sonnet *Silent Noon* is referred to at pp. 33–34.

p. 101. JENNY. The first draft of this belongs also to the 1847 period. In November 1860 Rossetti wrote to Allingham:

Would you tell me, as regards *Jenny* (which I reckon the most serious thing I have written), whether there is any objection you see in the treatment, or any side of the subject left untouched which ought to be included?

(*Letters of D. G. Rossetti to William Allingham*, p. 257.) See also Introduction pp. 28–30 and the Buchanan-Rossetti controversy, pp. 182–187.

p. 114. SONNETS FOR PICTURES. The corresponding pictures will be found at pp. 113 and 112 respectively.

p. 115, **Christina Rossetti**

b. 1830, younger sister of D. G. Rossetti. Began writing poetry in her teens; contributed to *The Germ* under pseudonym of Ellen Alleyn. Published *inter alia*: *Goblin Market and other Poems*, illustrated by D. G. Rossetti (1864); *Sing-Song*, a volume of poems for children, illustrated by Arthur Hughes (see pp. 119–120) (1872); *Speaking Likenesses*, a prose tale for children, also illustrated by Hughes (1874). Engaged to James Collinson (see pp. 196–197) but never married. Died 1894. A great part of her work is devotional poetry, but she is represented here only by lyrics which are notably Pre-Raphaelite in tone or were illustrated by Pre-Raphaelite painters. There is an essay on her by Virginia Woolf in *The Common Reader: Second Series* (London, 1932), and a biography, *The Life of Christina Rossetti*, by Mary F. Sandars (London, 1930).

p. 120, **William Allingham**

b. Ballyshannon 1824. Bank clerk and customs official. Ardent collector of Irish folk songs and ballads. Came to London 1847, and held various professional appointments in England. Edited poems of Edgar Allen Poe 1857. Retired from customs 1870 to become sub-editor of *Fraser's Magazine* under Froude, succeeding him as chief editor 1874; married same year. Died 1889. Intimate personal friend of D. G. Rossetti: see *Letters of Dante Gabriel Rossetti to William Allingham, 1854–70*, edited by G. Birkbeck Hill (London, 1897). Published various volumes of poetry from 1850 onward, most comprehensive being *Songs, Ballads, and Stories* (1877). Many of his poems are lyrics for traditional Irish airs or are based on Irish legends of fairies and the supernatural, the best-known being *Up the Airy Mountain*. His work must have had much to do with W. B. Yeats's delight in Pre-Raphaelitism. Rossetti's illustration to *The Maids of Elfin-Mere* is at p. 113; See also *William Allingham: A Diary*, edited by H. Allingham and D. Radford (London, 1907), and *Letters to William Allingham*, edited by H. Allingham and E. Baumer Williams (London, 1911).

p. 123, **William Bell Scott**
 For biographical and bibliographical notes see pp. 201–202.
Both these poems are from *Poems* (1875), which was illustrated by the author and Alma-Tadema.

p. 124. THE WITCH'S BALLAD. braw=handsome, gowden= golden, miminy=demure, unco' gleg=very sharp, stour=dust, cramoisie=crimson cloth, ayont=beyond, wame=stomach. Tansy and madwort are common herbs; agramie is not given either by the *N.E.D.* or the *English Dialect Dictionary*.

p. 127, **Thomas Woolner**
b. 1825. Student at R.A. Schools 1842, member of P.R.B. 1848. Contributed poetry to *The Germ* 1850. Emigrated to Australia 1852 (see note on F. M. Brown at pp. 198–199), returning 1854. Executed many statues, busts, and medallions, among his best-known being a bas-relief plaque of Tennyson. Published *My Beautiful Lady* (1863), a volume of poems based on the two poems *My Beautiful Lady* and *Of My Lady in Death*, originally published in *The Germ* No. 1, with the addition of many others. The six stanzas published here come from the first of the two *Germ* poems, which runs to thirty stanzas in all and is poetically very uneven. The first of the selected stanzas was illustrated by *Hunt* in *The Germ* (as reproduced here), and the sixth by Millais, but this drawing was not published. Died 1892.

p. 129, **William Morris**
 For biographical and bibliographical notes see p. 201.

p. 129. THE LIFE AND DEATH OF JASON. Published 1867, this was the first of Morris's long narrative poems. The passage comes from the beginning of the final book, Book XVII.

p. 130. THE EARTHLY PARADISE (1868–70). Contains a prologue and epilogue and twenty-four tales, two for each month of the year, one of each pair being of classical origin and the other from a non-classical source, often Northern. This poem is prefixed to the book.

p. 132 THE DEFENCE OF GUENEVERE. Title poem of a volume published 1858, from which all the remaining poems in this section are taken. See *Athenaeum* review at pp. 175–176.

p. 153. THE STORY OF THE UNKNOWN CHURCH. The first of Morris's stories to be published. Appeared in *The Oxford and Cambridge Magazine* 1856. Should be read in conjunction with his lecture *Gothic Architecture* (1889) and the passage at pp. 59–65 of the present volume.

p. 163. THE STORY OF THE GLITTERING PLAIN. The earliest of the prose romances dealing with an imaginary world of adventure that occupied Morris's last years; written 1890, it was the first book printed at the Kelmscott Press when it opened in 1891. See frontispiece. This passage comes from chapter vii; the vivid visualization of the scene is a tribute to his familiarity with Old Norse sagas.

p. 165, **Algernon Charles Swinburne**
b. 1837. Educated Eton and Oxford, became friendly with Rossetti, Morris, and Burne-Jones. Published *Atalanta in Calydon*, a verse tragedy, 1865, and *Poems and Ballads: First Series* (from which all these poems are taken) 1866. Admired Shelley and Baudelaire, whose work influenced him greatly, and the Elizabethan drama. Published poetry, dramas, and critical works on Blake, Elizabethan drama, etc. Anti-Christian and sensual note of his poetry occasioned much hostility: see Buchanan at pp. 176–179 and 187. Died 1909. The standard biographical and critical work is *Swinburne*, by Georges Lafourcade (1932). The poems are reproduced by courtesy of Messrs William Heinemann, Ltd.

THE CONTEMPORARY VIEW OF PRE-RAPHAELITISM

p. 174. A CRITICISM OF MILLAIS' "CHRIST IN THE HOUSE OF HIS PARENTS." FROM *Household Words*, June 15, 1850, in an article entitled "Old Lamps for New Ones."

p. 175. *The Athenaeum*: issue dated April 3, 1858.

p. 176, **Robert Buchanan**
b. Scotland 1841. Came to London as a writer and made an early reputation by his *London Poems* (1866). Published other volumes of poems, plays, and novels, but his reputation declined in his own lifetime and he is now remembered chiefly as the critic of Rossetti and Swinburne. Died 1901. A more fully documented account of this controversy and its relation to Buchanan's career

will be found in *Proceedings of the Modern Language Association of America*, vol. lxvii, No. 2 (March 1952), pp. 65–93: *Robert Buchanan and the Fleshly Controversy*, by John A. Cassidy.

p. 177. *Simeon Solomon* (1840–1905). London Jewish painter and poet much influenced by Rossetti and Swinburne; led a Bohemian life, and has much in common with the Æsthetic Movement of the 1890's.

p. 177. *his own great model*. Presumably Chaucer, of whom Buchanan speaks appreciatively elsewhere in this essay.

p. 182. *Jenny*. In a note to the 1872 reprint of this essay Buchanan quotes a review of this poem from *The Quarterly* which substantiates his own criticism.

p. 184. THE STEALTHY SCHOOL OF CRITICISM: see *The Athenæum*, December 16, 1871, pp. 792–794.

p. 188, **Walter Pater**
  b. 1839. Educated at Oxford; became Fellow of Brasenose College and remained a scholarly recluse until his death in 1894. A man of wide and deep culture whose writings and whose æsthetic principles had considerable influence on writers of the 1880's and 1890's. His main publications were: *Studies in the History of the Renaissance* (1873); *Marius the Epicurean*, a novel (1885), *Imaginary Portraits* (1887), *Appreciations* (1889), and *Miscellaneous Studies*, posthumously (1895). For critical works see: A. C. Benson, *Walter Pater* (London, 1906), G. Tillotson, *Criticism and the Nineteenth Century* (London, 1951), and T. S. Eliot, "The Place of Pater" in *The Eighteen Eighties*, edited by W. de la Mare (Cambridge, 1930).

p. 188. DANTE GABRIEL ROSSETTI. This essay, written in 1883, was not published until 1889 in *Appreciations*. That volume also included *Æsthetic Poetry*, an essay written in 1868, but this was omitted in the 1890 reprint and has not been republished since.

NOTES TO ILLUSTRATIONS
(Listed alphabetically by artists)

Ford Madox Brown
  For biographical and bibliographical notes see p. 198
p. 97. WORK: canvas, 53 x 77⅛ (1852–65). Discussed at pp. 22–25, and 51–58 above. Reproduced by kind permission of the Trustees of the Manchester City Art Gallery.

Sir Edward Coley Burne-Jones

b. Birmingham 1833. Met Morris at Exeter College, Oxford, 1853. Rossetti's *The Maids of Elfin-Mere* (*q.v.*) led to his determination to paint instead of entering the Church. Worked with Rossetti from 1856, helped with decoration of the Oxford Union 1857; visited Italy 1859 and again in 1862 with Ruskin. Designed stained glass and tapestries for Morris's firm, and also illustrated various Kelmscott Press volumes. Received baronetcy 1894, died 1898. See *Edward Burne-Jones: a Record and Review*, by Malcolm Bell (London, 1892; revised 1898 and title changed to *Sir Edward Burne-Jones*, etc.).

p. 41 and p. 151. TROILUS AND CRISEYDE and CRISEYDE SEES TROILUS RETURN. These illustrations are taken from *Troilus and Criseyde* in the Kelmscott Chaucer, published 1896. The first illustrates Book III, stanza 26, and the second Book II, stanzas 90–95. The stylization of figure in the first with its suggestion of Beardsley indicates affinities between late Pre-Raphaelitism and the Æsthetic movement of the 1890's. Photographs kindly supplied by the City of Birmingham Museum and Art Gallery.

p. 132 and p. 172. CUPID FINDING PSYCHE ASLEEP IN HER GARDEN and PSYCHE WADING ACROSS THE STREAM. As early as 1865 Morris and Burne-Jones planned an illustrated edition of *The Earthly Paradise*. Burne-Jones made seventy designs for the *Story of Cupid and Psyche*, a theme to which he often returned in later years, and of these fifty-four were engraved on wood mostly by Morris himself. The scheme was abandoned in 1868. The designs for these were given by Ruskin to the Ruskin School of Drawing at Oxford, and twenty-four woodcuts from them illustrated the Gregynog Press edition of Robert Bridges's version of the story in 1935. A complete set of the original woodcuts is owned by the City of Birmingham Museum and Art Gallery, by whose kind permission these are reproduced. An extract from Morris's poem to which the first of these relates will be found at pp. 131–132.

Arthur Hughes

b. 1830. Admitted to R.A. Schools 1847. Converted to Pre-Raphaelitism by *The Germ* 1850. Worked with Rossetti on Oxford Union murals 1857. Regular exhibitor at Academy. Died 1915. His easel pictures, such as *April Love* (inspired by a quotation from Tennyson's *The Miller's Daughter*), often have a literary source, but achieve a delightful freshness, feeling, and poetry which characterize his drawings as well.

p. 119. This drawing is taken from Christina Rossetti's *Sing-Song* (1872), where it illustrates the poem printed below it here. Hughes also illustrated one of Allingham's poems in *Day and Night Songs* (1855).

William Holman Hunt
For biographical and bibliographical notes see pp. 200–201

p. 68. THE LADY OF SHALOTT: from the Moxon edition of Tennyson, 1857. Hunt (*Pre-Raphaelitism and the P.R.B.*, vol. ii, pp. 124–125) records Tennyson's disapproval of this: why, he asked Hunt, was "her hair wildly tossed about as if by a tornado?" and "Why did you make the web wind round and round her like the threads of a cocoon?" He believed that "an illustrator ought never to add anything to what he finds in the text." In 1889 Hunt executed a similar design in oils.

p. 72. THE BEGGAR MAID: also from the Moxon Tennyson. Here Tennyson objected to the steps (Hunt, *op. cit.*, p. 125) but not, apparently, to the curiously contorted posture. Despite this the drawing has a Pre-Raphaelite simplicity that contrasts pleasingly with Burne-Jones's *King Cophetua and the Beggar Maid*.

p. 96. THE AWAKENED CONSCIENCE: canvas, 29¾ x 21⅝. Exhibited 1854. See Introduction, pp. 25–31, and 36–37. Reproduced by kind permission of the owner, Sir Colin Anderson, from a photograph supplied by *The Studio*.

p. 128. MY BEAUTIFUL LADY (1850). This etching appeared in the first number of *The Germ* as illustration to Woolner's poem of the same name. It refers particularly to the lines quoted here.

Sir John Everett Millais
b. 1829. Entered R.A. Schools 1840. With Hunt and Rossetti founded P.R.B. 1848. Became A.R.A. 1853, R.A. 1863, baronet 1885, P.R.A. 1890. In 1855 married Ruskin's wife, Effie. Died 1896. His later work, popular rather than Pre-Raphaelite, has been frequently attacked for its facility and lack of taste, amounting at times almost to vulgarity, but his precociously manifested technical skill never failed him. See: J. G. Millais, *The Life and Letters of Sir John Everett Millais* (2 vols, 1899); M. H. Spielmann, *Millais and his Works* (1898).

p. 17. DORA. From the Moxon Tennyson, 1857.

> Then they clung about
> The old man's neck, and kiss'd him many times.
> And all the man was broken with remorse.

p. 35. LOCKSLEY HALL. Also from the Moxon Tennyson:

> Many an evening by the water did we watch the stately ships,
> And our spirits rush'd together at the touching of the lips.

p. 145. RETRIBUTION: pen and sepia ink, 8 x 10 (1854). See Introduction, p. 30. Present whereabouts of original unknown. Reproduced from photograph kindly loaned by the Phaidon Press, Ltd.

p. 161. CHRIST IN THE HOUSE OF HIS PARENTS: canvas, $33\frac{1}{2}$ x 54 (1849–50). See Introduction p. 34 and pp. 174–175 of text. Reproduced by courtesy of the Trustees of the Tate Gallery.

William Morris

For biographical and bibliographical notes see pp. 199–200.
Although it has not been possible to reproduce any of Morris's original designs here, his work at the Kelmscott Press is represented by the frontispiece, the opening page of the 1894 edition of *The Story of the Glittering Plain*. Photograph supplied by the Victoria and Albert Museum. Like much of the Kelmscott typography ornateness of letterpress and layout make a pleasing visual impression but are not easy reading.

Dante Gabriel Rossetti

For biographical and bibliographical notes see pp. 202–205.
p. 112. THE GIRLHOOD OF MARY VIRGIN: canvas, 33 x 25 (1849). See sonnets at pp. 114–115. Rossetti's first painting and the first publicly exhibited painting with the monogram PRB. Exhibited Hyde Park Gallery Free Exhibition 1849. The 'invention' of the Holy Dove on the trellis is parallelled by Millais in *Christ in the House of His Parents*, where the dove is perched on a ladder-rung, and the Crucifixion, prefigured by the blood in Millais' picture, is here suggested by the vine-covered trellis in front of St Joachim and the palm and briar crossed on the floor. Reproduced by courtesy of the Trustees of the Tate Gallery.

p. 113. DESIGN FOR FOUND: pen and ink, $9\frac{1}{4}$ x $8\frac{5}{8}$ (1853). See sonnet at p. 114. The models were Madox Brown and Fanny Cornforth. The oil painting of this was never completed.

p. 113. THE MAIDS OF ELFIN-MERE. Woodcut from Allingham's

Day and Night Songs (1855). See poem at p. 120 above, and note on Burne-Jones, p. 209. Rossetti's letters to Allingham reveal his dissatisfaction with Dalziel's cutting of the block, and a letter to his mother (W. M. Rossetti: *D. G. Rossetti: Letters and Memoir*, vol. ii, p. 139) describes the illustration as "one that used to be by me till it became the exclusive work of Dalziel who cut it." In spite of this it was Dalziel who cut his illustrations for the Moxon Tennyson. Reproduced by courtesy of the Trustees of the Tate Gallery.

p. 116–117. GOBLIN MARKET: woodcut (1861). Illustrates the lines from Christina Rossetti's poem printed below it here. Published 1862.

p. 144. JANE BURDEN AS QUEEN GUINEVERE: pen and ink, 19 x 15 (1858). Daughter of an Oxford business-man, Jane Burden became Morris's wife in 1859. She is also the model of his *La Belle Iseulte* (also sometimes known as *Guenevere*). See p. 33. Reproduced by courtesy of the Board of Governors and Guardians of the National Gallery of Ireland, Dublin.

p. 144. STUDY FOR THE BLESSED DAMOZEL: oil, 19 x 18 (1874). Rossetti completed two oil paintings of this theme, 1876–77 and 1879; both have predellas, showing the lover on earth, but the former with its groups of reunited lovers in the background is classed by Marillier as the better. This version, reproduced from a photograph kindly supplied by W. F. Mansell, was a study for the central figure. In 1875 Rossetti made a very lovely, but quite differently posed, study in red chalk. The poem is printed at pp. 81–85, and Buchanan's comments at pp. 179–182 should also be consulted.

p. 160. LAUNCELOT IN THE QUEEN'S CHAMBER: pen and black and brown ink, $10\frac{1}{4}$ x $13\frac{3}{4}$ (1857). Design for the Oxford Union decorations, but not carried out. Illustrates chapter clxix of the *Morte d'Arthur*. Compare Morris's *Defence of Guenevere* (pp. 132–143) and Introduction (p. 41).

This, and the design for *Found*, are reproduced by courtesy of the trustees of the City of Birmingham Art Gallery.

William Bell Scott

For biographical and bibliographical notes see pp. 201–202.

p. 123. STUDIES FROM NATURE. This illustration is taken from *Poems*, by W. B. Scott (1875), and is included for its characteristically Pre-Raphaelite use of natural detail. A number of poems in this volume are grouped under the title *Studies from Nature—*

among them *Green Cherries*, from which a passage is reprinted here.

Elizabeth Siddal

b. London 1834. A milliner's assistant discovered by the Pre-Raphaelite painter W. H. Deverell, and introduced to D. G. Rossetti, whose model she became and whom she married in 1860. Gave birth to still-born daughter 1861, died of an overdose of laudanum 1862. A woman of outstanding beauty but inclined to melancholia. Her paintings and poetry very closely resemble those of her husband but have a sensibility and intensity of their own. W. M. Rossetti published fifteen of her poems.

p. 145. PIPPA PASSES: pen and brown ink, $8\frac{1}{2}$ x $11\frac{1}{4}$. In January 1856 Rossetti writes to Allingham: "In London I showed Browning Miss Siddal's drawing from *Pippa Passes*, with which he was delighted beyond measure." It illustrates the passage in the second part of section iii of that work: "Pippa is passing from the Turret to the Bishop's brother's House close to the Duomo S. Maria. Poor girls sitting on the steps." Reproduced by kind permission of the owner, J. N. Bryson, Esq., from a photograph loaned by Mr John Gere.

CHRONOLOGICAL TABLE

1848 Foundation of the Pre-Raphaelite Brotherhood by Holman Hunt, D. G. Rossetti, and J. E. Millais.

1850 *January to May*: four numbers of *The Germ* (edited by W. M. Rossetti) appear.

Royal Academy Exhibition includes *Christ in the House of His Parents* (J. E. Millais) and other Pre-Raphaelite works.

Attacks begin in the Press.

Tennyson becomes Poet Laureate.

1851 *May 13 and May 30*: Ruskin writes to *The Times* in defence of Pre-Raphaelitism.

The Great Exhibition held in Hyde Park.

1852 Burne-Jones goes to Exeter College, Oxford.

1853 Morris goes to Exeter College, Oxford.

Millais elected A.R.A.

1853–56 The Crimean War.

1854 *May 5 and May 25*: Ruskin again writes to *The Times* about Pre-Raphaelite painting, especially Holman Hunt's.

1855 Allingham publishes *Day and Night Songs*, illustrated by D. G. Rossetti.

Morris and Burne-Jones leave Oxford.

Millais marries Ruskin's former wife.

1856 Ruskin, in *Notes on the R.A. Exhibition*, writes: "the battle is completely and confessedly won" by the P.R.B.

Swinburne goes to Balliol College, Oxford.

1857 The Moxon edition of Tennyson published, with illustrations by Rossetti, Millais, and Hunt.

Rossetti, Morris, Burne-Jones, and others undertake mural decoration of the Oxford Union.

1858 Morris publishes *The Defence of Guenevere and other Poems*.

1859 Morris marries Jane Burden.

Swinburne leaves Oxford.

1860 Rossetti marries Elizabeth Siddal.

1861 Rossetti publishes *Early Italian Poets*.

Firm of Morris, Marshall, and Faulkner founded.

1862 Christina Rossetti publishes *Goblin Market and other Poems*, illustrated by Rossetti.

Death of Rossetti's wife.

1863 Millais elected R.A.

In Paris *Salon des Refusés* marks beginning of Impressionism.

1866 Swinburne publishes *Poems and Ballads: First Series*.

Christina Rossetti publishes *The Prince's Progress and other Poems*, illustrated by Rossetti.

1868–70 Morris publishes *The Earthly Paradise*.

1870 Rossetti publishes *Poems*.

The Franco-Prussian War.

1871 Buchanan publishes *The Fleshly School of Poetry*, and Rossetti replies.

1872 Christina Rossetti publishes *Sing-Song*, illustrated by Arthur Hughes.

1881 Rossetti publishes *Ballads and Sonnets*.

1882 Death of D. G. Rossetti.

1885 Millais receives baronetcy.

1882–90 Morris's most active period of Socialist work in pamphlets, poems, and lectures.

1889 Pater publishes *Appreciations*, with essays on Rossetti and on Æsthetic Poetry.

Death of Allingham.

1890 Morris founds the Kelmscott Press, publishes *News from Nowhere*, and begins the writing of his long prose romances.

Death of Bell Scott.

Millais elected P.R.A.

1892 Morris refuses Laureateship on death of Tennyson.

Death of Woolner.

1893 Death of Madox Brown

1894 Death of Christina Rossetti.

Burne-Jones receives baronetcy.

1896 Death of Morris and Millais.

1898 Death of Burne-Jones.

1905 Holman Hunt awarded O.M.

1907 Death of F. G. Stephens.

1909 Death of Swinburne.

1910 Death of Holman Hunt.

1919 Death of W. M. Rossetti.

BIBLIOGRAPHY

NOTE. Texts and works of criticism on individual authors have been listed under that author's name in the notes, and, to save space, are not repeated here.

The Pre-Raphaelites

(Works marked with an asterisk are illustrated.)

*BATE, PERCY: *The English Pre-Raphaelite Painters* (London, 1901).
*GAUNT, WILLIAM: *The Pre-Raphaelite Tragedy* (London, 1942). Reprinted 1943 as *The Pre-Raphaelite Dream*.
HOUGH, GRAHAM: *The Last Romantics* (London, 1949).
*HUNT, W. HOLMAN: *Pre-Raphaelitism and the Pre-Raphaelites Brotherhood* (New York, 1905–6, 2 vols.).
*IRONSIDE, ROBIN, and GERE, JOHN: *Pre-Raphaelite Painters* (London, 1948).
*JAMES, PHILIP: *English Book Illustration, 1800–1900* (London and New York, 1947).
RUSKIN, JOHN: *Pre-Raphaelitism* (London, 1851).

The Literary Background

BATHO, EDITH, and DOBREE, BONAMY: *The Victorians and After* (London, 1938; revised 1950).
ELTON, OLIVER: *Survey of English Literature, 1830–80* (London, 1920).
EVANS, B. IFOR: *English Poetry in the Later Nineteenth Century* (London, 1933).
TILLOTSON, G.: *Criticism and the Nineteenth Century* (London, 1951).

The Social and Historical Background

TREVELYAN, G. M.: *British History in the Nineteenth Century, 1782–1901* (London, 1922).
English Social History (London, 1944).
YOUNG, G. M.: *Early Victorian England, 1830–65* (London, 1934).
Victorian England: Portrait of an Age (London, 1936).

Personalities and Thought of the Age

MASSINGHAM, H. J. and H. W.: *The Great Victorians* (London, 1932).
BRITISH BROADCASTING CORPORATION: *Ideas and Beliefs of the Victorians* (London, 1949).